Editor:

Dona Herweck Rice

Senior Editor:

Sharon Coan, M.S. Ed.

Art Direction:

Elayne Roberts

Product Manager:

Phil Garcia

Imaging:

Alfred Lau

Consultant:

Sandra D. Lowry
Executive Director
Indian Education Center
Susanville, CA

Publishers:

Rachelle Cracchiolo, M.S. Ed.

Mary Dupuy Smith, M.S. Ed.

PRIMARY

Native Ame
Arts and Cultures
Exploring Tradition

D0600490

Author and Illustrator:
Mary E. Connors

Teacher Created Materials, Inc.
P.O. Box 1040
Huntington Beach, CA 92647
©1994 Teacher Created Materials, Inc.
Made in U.S.A.

ISBN-1-55734-619-4

Table of Contents

Table of Contents (cont.)

Introduction to Native American Arts and Culture

When the first Europeans arrived on the shores of North America more than five hundred years ago, over twenty million Native Americans were living across the American continents. The native people spoke more than four hundred dialects and used sophisticated universal forms of communication. Their long established trade routes acted as "cultural corridors" among the people.

In the area which was to become the United States, ancient footpaths crisscrossed the continent. Well-tended gardens of fruits, vegetables, and grains stretched across the woodlands and deserts, where elaborate irrigation channels linked many settlements. Large towns of wooden homes and lodges provided safe and fruitful living for many. Children played games of all kinds and were taught the history of their people by the elders who sang and danced the stories around the sacred fire. Drums, flutes, rattles, and fans carried their prayers to the thousands of deities who created Mother Earth and the plants, animals, and humans living harmoniously there. The songs and dances were requests to continue their lives as their ancestors had for hundreds of generations, walking forever on "The Beautiful Path."

The quest of Native Americans has always been to live in harmony with the world. Land, water, plants, animals, and air were considered endless treasures, yet they belonged to no one. Instead, everyone belonged to the land and was a caretaker of the earth. This is the meaning of "The Beautiful Path." It is a celebration of living still valued by many Native Americans today.

The philosophy of death is consistent with the philosophy of life. Traditionally, there is no death, but merely a passage between worlds. All living things return to the earth in another form once their spirits leave their physical bodies. The spirit world is known as "The True World."

Most Native American groups call themselves by names that translate to "the People." "Indians" is a name given by Christopher Columbus, a European. His mistaken belief that he had reached India was merely the first of a long line of misunderstandings supported and perpetuated by Europeans.

The legacy of the rich Native American cultures has contributed greatly to the uniqueness of contemporary American culture. The American founding father, Benjamin Franklin, often spoke respectfully of the Iroquois Confederacy of Nations. He formulated his revolutionary plan for a democratic nation (free from the dictates of European monarchy) upon the structure of the Confederacy, which sought to unite all societies by the pledge of peace. Ironically, the Confederacy was intentionally broken by the Europeans in their determination to transform the "wild frontier" of the new United States into "tamed territories."

The history of Native Americans is not static, nor is it all past. Many descendants of the ancient societies continue the traditions and values of their ancestors. It is important to remember that though this book focuses on the People of the past, Native Americans are living and thriving today, part of the modern world yet ever-mindful of their ancestries.

Note: The activities in this book, though based on tradition, often employ non-traditional materials.

Cultural Areas in This Book

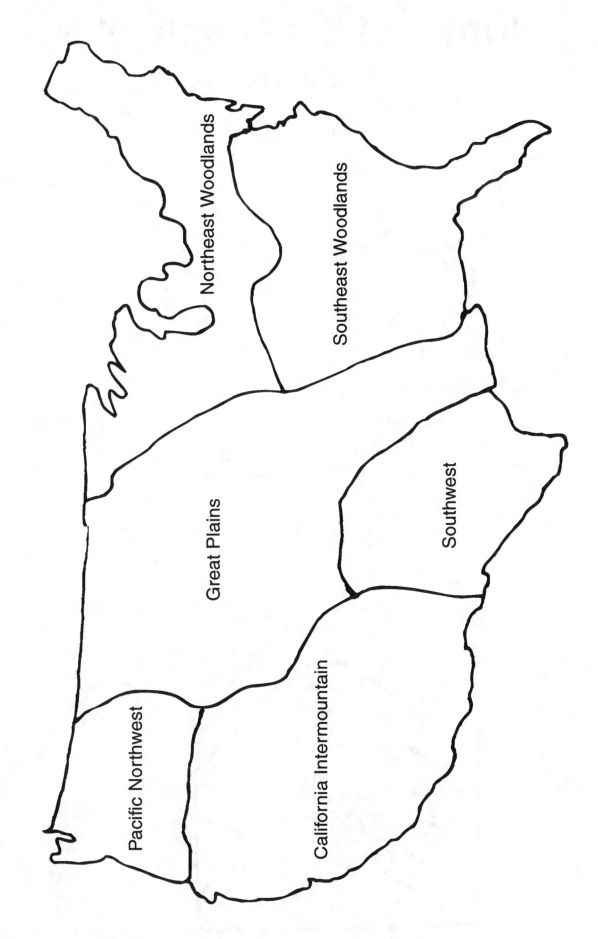

Names of the People of North America

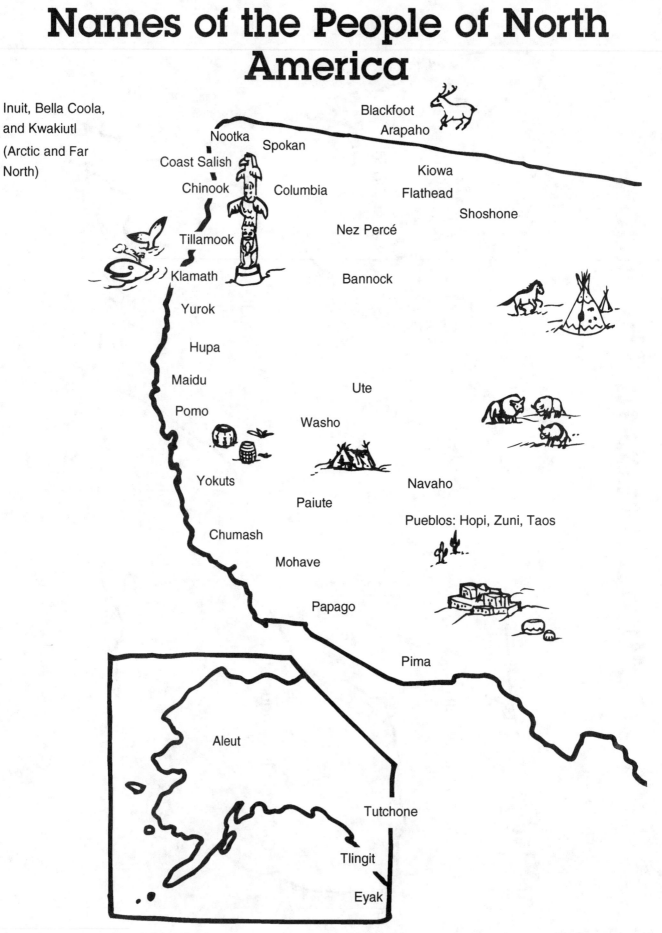

Inuit, Bella Coola, and Kwakiutl (Arctic and Far North)

Blackfoot
Arapaho
Nootka
Spokan
Coast Salish
Kiowa
Chinook
Columbia
Flathead
Shoshone
Nez Percé
Tillamook
Klamath
Bannock
Yurok
Hupa
Maidu
Ute
Pomo
Washo
Yokuts
Navaho
Paiute
Pueblos: Hopi, Zuni, Taos
Chumash
Mohave
Papago
Pima
Aleut
Tutchone
Tlingit
Eyak

Names of the People of North America *(cont.)*

Cree

Gros Ventre

Crow

Hidatsa

Mandan

Ojibwa

Menominee

Winnebago

Fox

Oto

Iowa

Cheyenne

Arikara

Pawnee

Kansa

Witchita

Missouri

Osage

Caddo

Natchez

Potawatomi

Huron

Algonquin

Montagnais

Micmak

Abnaki

Penobscot

Delaware

Iroquois

Erie

Susquehannock

Powhatan

Miami

Omaha

Shawnee

Cherokee

Tuscarora

Chickasaw

Creek

Choctaw

Timuca

Calusa

Forests of the United States

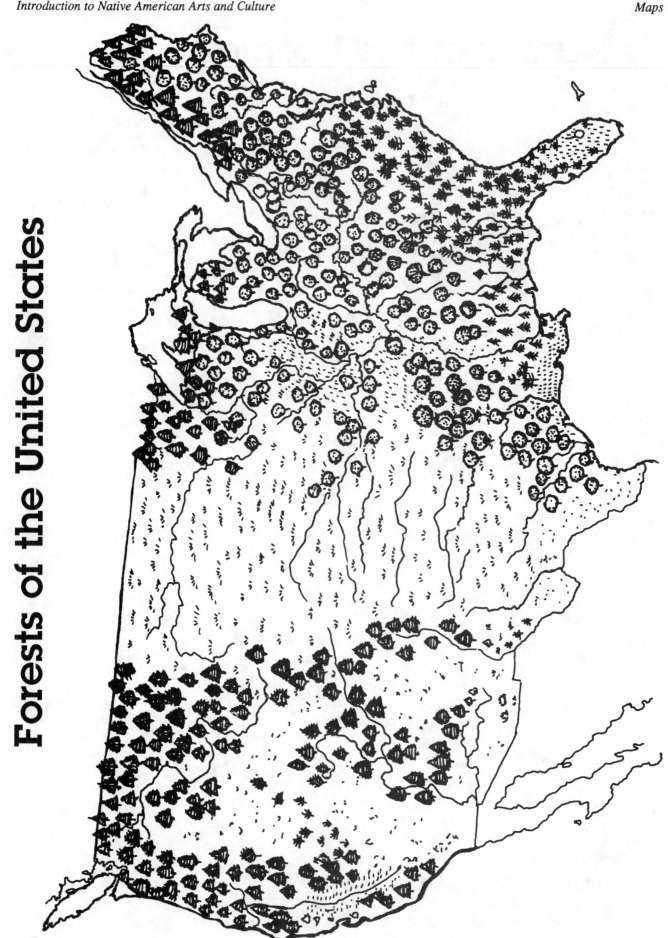

Rivers and Mountains of the United States

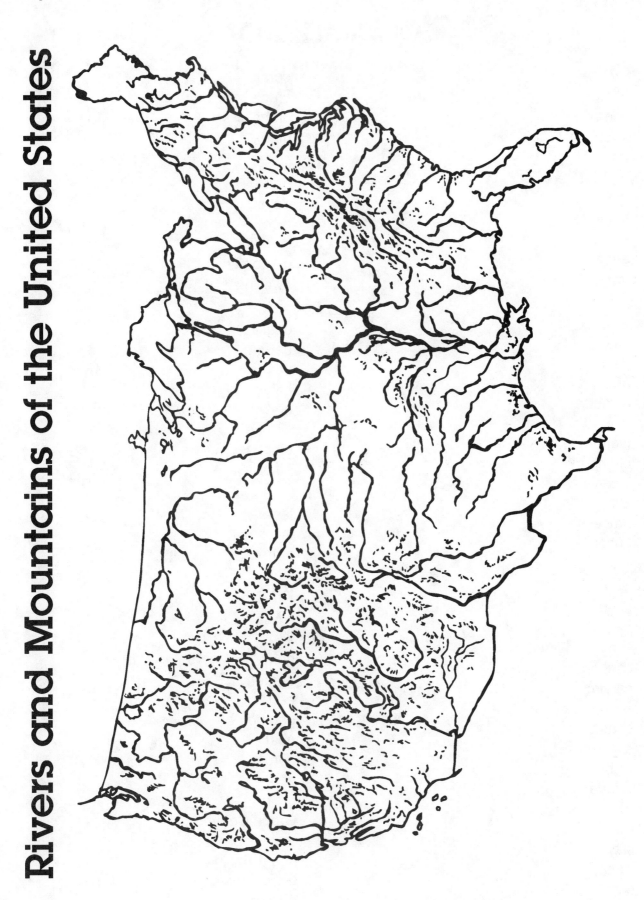

Vocabulary

Aa

abalone
acorn
adobe
adze
agriculture
amulet
antelope
Arctic
arrow
awl
axe

Bb

badger
bark
beaver
blubber
bow
bighorn sheep
birchbark
bison
blade
bracelet
buffalo

Cc

cactus
candlefish
canoe
canyon
caribou
carving
ceremony
charcoal
chestnut
chief
cicada
clam shell
clan
clay
climate
coil
conch shell

coral
cradleboard
crane
creek

Dd

deer
desert
dice
dolphin
dragonfly
dwelling

Ee

eagle
earring
east
effigy
elk
elm tree
emboss
embroidery

Ff

festival
fetish
fir tree
flint
fort
fox

Gg

game
garden
garter
geometric
goat
gorget
gourd
grain
Grand Canyon
grasshopper
Great Basin
Great Lakes
grinding stone
gum

Vocabulary *(cont.)*

Hh

Haida
hairpiece
halibut
harpoon
hawk
headdress
hickory nut
hogan

Ii

Ice Age
igloo
inlay
iron
irrigation
ivory
ivy

Jj

jade
javelin
jewelry
juniper tree

Kk

kachina
kayak
kiva

Ll

lace
lance
lead
leather
legend
leggings
lightning
lizard
loom

Mm

maize
mask
mastodon
melon

mesa
migrate
milling stone
mink
moccasin
mortar
mosaic
mountain lion
mulberry
myth

Nn

nature
necklace
needle
nomad
north

Oo

oak tree
obsidian
octopus
oil
opossum
otter
owl

Pp

paddle
paint
pendant
petroglyph
pine tree
piñon tree
plains
poplar tree
porcupine
pottery
pouch
prairie
priest
priestess
pueblo

Vocabulary *(cont.)*

Qq

quail
quest
quill
quiver

Rr

rake
rattle
rattlesnake
raven
red ochre
reindeer
religion
rosette

Ss

sagebrush
saguaro
salmon
sandpainting
sandstone
scraper
scroll
seal
seaweed
shaman
shark
sheepshell
shield
slate
sled
sling
sloth
south
spindle
spiral
spruce tree
squash
stampede
straw
sunflower

Tt

tablet
tattoo
temple
tepee (tipi; teepee)
textile
thunder
thunderbird
tobacco
toboggan
tomb
totem pole
trade
travois
trophy
trout
turkey
turquoise
twine

Uu

Utah
utensils
umiak boat

Vv

valley
village
vision

Ww

walnut
walrus
wampum belt
warp
weave
weft
whale
willow tree
wolf
woodpecker

Xx, Yy, Zz

yucca

12

Homes and Lodges

The Earliest Homes

The North American continent spans an area of over 7,000 square miles (11,000 square kilometers). Immigrants from Europe and Asia immigrated to this enormous continent over the centuries, and the population grew until, by the time of Christopher Columbus, there were millions of people living across the land from Alaska to South America.

The earliest Americans, ancestors of contemporary Native Americans, lived in the cold and harsh climate of the Ice Age. Hunters depended upon the large animals grazing along the edge of the ice flows for the meat and fur they could provide. To make a shelter from the cold winds and snow, the furs of animals were fastened to poles of wood or bones. The earliest Americans had the knowledge of fire and made fires in their dwellings and temporary shelters. As the climate became warmer over time, the people began to change their lifestyles to adapt to the new conditions. They also adapted to their particular environment so that homes in one area were possibly quite different from homes in another area.

Adapting to the Environment

The human species is very adaptable to a wide range of habitat and climatic conditions. Humans have survived the hottest deserts and the coldest tundra. They have made permanent and temporary dwellings from wood, bark, animal skins, grass, thatch, mud, and stone, each providing the shelter they needed. Homes were always made from the materials available in each area. In the coldest Arctic, the people built their homes from animal furs, wood, or blocks of ice. In forested areas, homes and lodges were made from planks of wood. Homes were permanent or temporary depending upon the lifestyle and the season.

Homes Today

Most of the homes in North America today are permanent dwellings, and they are usually quite different from the homes of the past. Even mobile homes are usually parked for years at a time, and some camper vehicles are used as homes. Today, as in the past, there can be a sharp contrast in the housing styles across America. From the city highrise apartments to the isolated homes of the countryside, Americans live alone, with family groups, or with friends, just as they always have. In any of these modern homes, you might find a Native American.

Make sure the students know that the People today usually live in houses that are just like everyone else's. However, to better understand the Native American homes of yesterday, they may enjoy hearing about the different styles of homes made centuries ago. They can make some traditional Native American homes with paper and clay, discuss their present day homes, and then design homes for the future. They can also color, cut out, and put together the minibook on pages 21-23.

Topics for Discussion

Discuss the various styles of homes and public buildings found in your town, state, and country. Homes in other parts of the world may be reviewed as well. The students may be surprised to see the similarities they will find.

Use some or all of the following questions for discussion topics.

1. Where do we live?
2. Why do we live in a building?
3. What materials were used to make your home? The school? The local library?
4. Where did these materials come from?
5. Who built your home? Could one person build it alone?
6. What is the shape of your home? The school? The nearest fire department?
7. What kind of homes did the Native Americans have?

   (tepees, reed houses, stone houses, adobe, wigwams, etc.)

8. What were the Native American homes of long ago made from?

   (stones, woven reeds, mud bricks, redwood, buffalo skins, cedar planks, etc.)

9. What size and shape were the traditional Native American homes?

   (The sizes and shapes varied depending on the region, climate, permanency of the dwelling, and the available materials.)

10. Who built the traditional Native American homes? Could one person build a home without help?

    (Answers will vary depending on the home cultural group building it.)

11. Were any of the traditional Native American homes apartment houses?

    (The pueblo dwellings of the Southwest were a type of apartment house complex.)

12. Are any traditional Native American houses still made?

    (Yes, some are made for practical purposes as well as for purposes of keeping tradition alive.)

Kwakiutl Northwest Plank House Pop-Up

Directions: Color and cut out the plank house and boat on the dotted lines. Fold the house and boat as shown to make a pop-up.

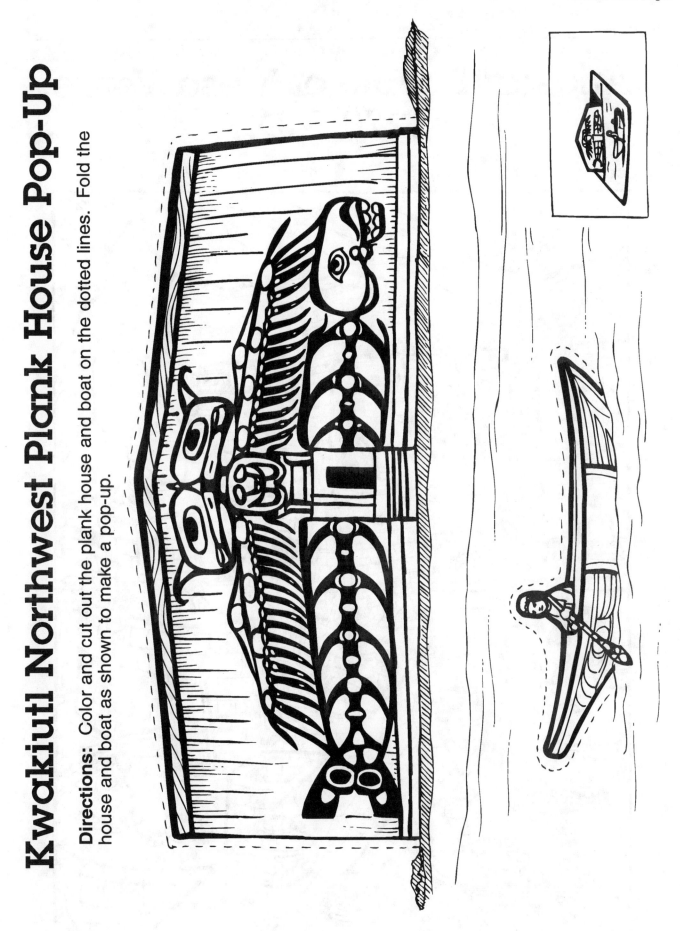

Name _____

Anasazi Pueblo of Mesa Verde, 1270 A.D.

Directions: Color the picture.

16

Name _____

Match the Home

Directions: Cut out each home and paste it in the correct habitat.

Southwest Pueblo Pop-Up

Directions: Cut the dotted lines only. Fold the picture as shown to make a pop-up.

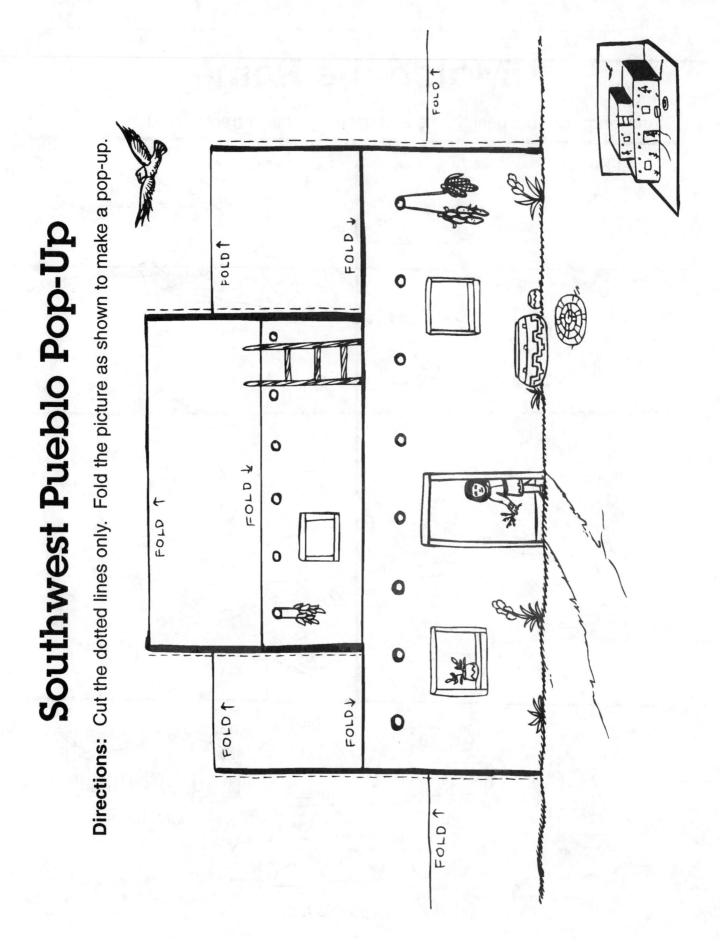

Great Plains Tepee

Directions: Color and cut out the tepee. Tape the sides together as shown.

Making Homes

Southwest Pueblo Apartment House

Materials: milk cartons, shoeboxes, scissors, clay, sand, and glue

Directions: Attach the boxes and milk cartons with glue. Cut windows and doors in the boxes. Cover the building with clay and sand. Use sticks to make the roof beams and ladders.

Arctic Igloo

Materials: sugar cubes, icing*, cardboard, and wax paper

Directions: Cover the cardboard with waxed paper. Make a circle on the cardboard with sugar cubes. Build up a dome over the circle with sugar cubes and icing. The icing will be the glue that holds the cubes together, and it can also be used as "snow."

*(To make a good, stiff icing, mix 2 egg whites, 1/2 tsp. [2.5mL] cream of tartar, and 3 cups [750 mL] powdered sugar)

Traditional Native American Dwellings and Shelters

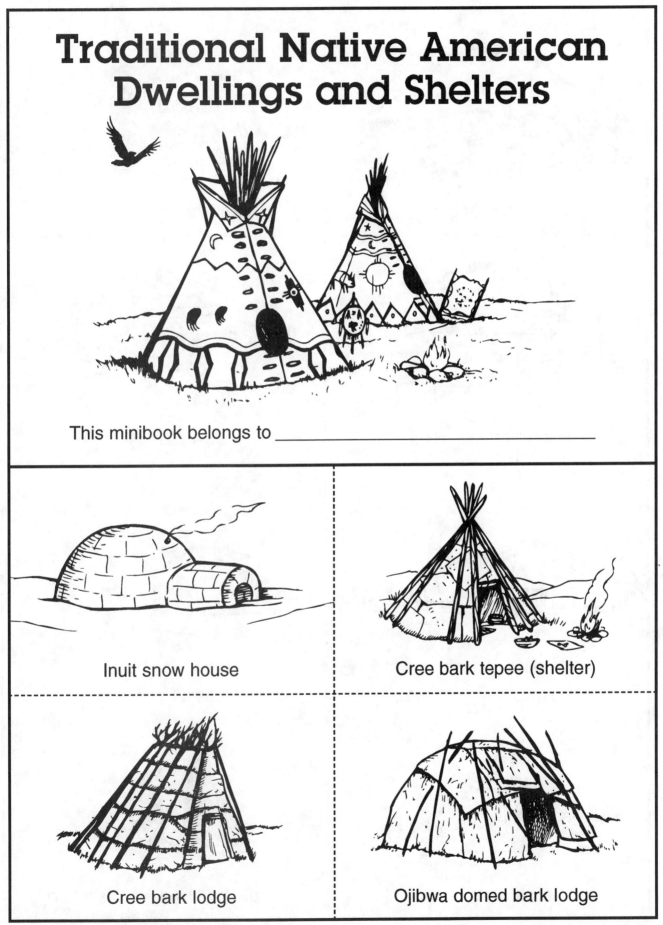

This minibook belongs to _____

Inuit snow house

Cree bark tepee (shelter)

Cree bark lodge

Ojibwa domed bark lodge

Navaho hogan

Apache brush lodge

Pueblo adobe village

Miwok round house

Kwakiutl plank house

Haida plank house

Salish earth house

Paiute brush wickiup (shelter)

Sioux buffalo-hide tepee

Woodlands bark house

Omaha earth lodge

Wichita grass house

Kickapoo wigwam

Iroquois long house

Seminole summer house

Creek house

Quest for Food

Notes for the Teacher

This chapter explores the hunting, gathering, cultivating, storing, and preparing of food by early Native Americans. While studying the chapter, keep in mind that this book as a whole focuses primarily on the Native Americans of previous centuries. It is important for students to understand that the People are living today as modernly as everyone else, though collectively they try to keep their traditions alive.

Food for Life

It is possible that the first people entering North America thousands of years ago were following the ice age caribou, mastodon, and other large mammals which grazed on the grassy fields at the edge of the glacier flows. The destiny of humans has always depended upon the availability of edible plants and animals as a food supply. Without food, physical strength soon diminishes, making all other concerns seem unimportant. There can be no life without food.

Food as the Basis for Culture

All people devote a great amount of time and effort in order to obtain, store, and prepare food. Every culture possesses traditional cuisine as well as techniques and taboos regarding the gathering, hunting, cultivating, storing, and preparing of food. Moreover, culture is allowed to develop when an abundant food supply permits leisure time for the people to explore areas of interest. Surplus time allows each person to focus on arts such as storytelling, dance, drama, painting, sculpture, pottery, and basketry.

These art forms are the vital record of human culture. The earliest known cave art in Europe depicts deer and bison being hunted by humans with spears. Some believe that this suggests the paintings and carvings were created in order to ensure a successful hunt. The earliest known dances and prayers in North America were requests for good hunting. The seasonal kachina dances of the Southwest are directly tied to the planting and harvesting cycle. The dances request rainfall and an excellent harvest of the bean, melon, squash, and corn fields. When the harvest arrives, feasts, songs, and dances of thankfulness are enjoyed by everyone. Many cultures share legends which explain the origin of animals and plants which supply their food.

Food and the Family

In many households today, as in the past, food is a central focus of the family unit. Mealtimes may be the only time when the entire family group gathers. Holidays and special events are closely associated with favorite foods, and plenty of them. Without food at these gatherings, much of the reason for festivity would be gone.

Quest for Food (cont.)

Food in the Modern Age

In modern North America, many people take an abundant food supply for granted. The fruits, vegetables, grains, and meats seem to appear without effort in supermarkets, school cafeterias, and refrigerators. The origin and processing of the food is a mystery for many people. When the food runs out, there is always more at the store. Unless people are directly involved with the farming or harvesting of food, there is limited appreciation for the origin, time, effort, and resources which are necessary to ensure a steady food supply. If they were suddenly forced to hunt, gather, and cultivate their own food, such people would be surprised at the intensive labor required to achieve this most basic necessity of all living creatures.

The Earth Balance

For thousands of years, millions of Native Americans gathered, hunted, cultivated, and prepared food of many kinds. The earth provided for them, and in return, they cared for the earth with a sense of brotherhood and responsibility. The People saw themselves as the caretakers of the land, not its owners or rulers. They believed that all living things belong to the earth and have a place in its state of balance. Plants provide people with food, fibers for weaving, soap, tea, medicinal herbs, and natural dyes for porcupine quills, feathers, fur, and paints. Animals provide food and materials for clothing, shelter, cooking, and so forth.

For Native Americans, the earth has always been seen as a beautiful mother spirit who supports all her children. Plants, animals, and humans share a common ancestry and a common fate. All living things are interdependent, which means they need one another for survival. Earth, sky, water, air, plants, animals, and people are connected. If one plant or animal species is out of balance, the entire earth suffers for it. Nothing is useless. Even weeds have their place.

The Creator Spirits and Divine Purpose

The Native Americans believed that everything—the sun, moon, stars, plants, animals, rivers, mountains, and people—were sacred, as they were placed here by the wise creator spirits. Even if one was not sure of a particular species' lifestyle or the possible uses for a specific plant, it was assumed that the creator spirits knew its purpose and reason for existence. All the earth was a sacred field, the most precious gift from the creator spirits who shared their wisdom of The Beautiful Path with humans.

The needs of future generations were always considered. Therefore, no one took more than needed from Mother Earth, and no one lived through a single day without offering prayers and gifts of thankfulness for the gifts from Mother Earth and the spiritual force which permeates and sustains all that is seen and unseen.

Quest for Food (cont.)

Cooking with Stones

Cooking was done in several ways. Open pit fires were dug into the ground and lined with stones. Some foods were wrapped in corn husks or leaves and cooked under the hot ashes. Meat, fish, and stew were commonly cooked in waterproof baskets, wooden boxes of cedar, elm, or birchbark, or in large pottery jars, depending on the area. Metal cooking kettles came with the advent of European traders. Stones were heated in the fire and then dropped into the cooking vessel filled with water, meat, and vegetables. The hot stones would quickly bring the water to a boil and the food would be cooked. Small stones which were round and smooth were preferred for cooking in this manner. Hot coals from the fires were carried in clamshells and other fireproof containers. (Note: Coals could be carried from camp to camp in this manner as well.)

Food Storage

Whether harvested, gathered, or hunted, food needed to be stored. Fish and meat were cut into strips and dried in the sun or smoked over a fire. Pemmican, a favorite food in the Great Plains, was made from crushed nuts, berries, and meat and then carried in a parfleche, a rawhide, envelope-like container. These were decorated with paintings and porcupine quill patterns. The parfleche was tied shut with thin strips of sinew. The Iroquois people loved apples and grew them in large orchards. Apples and other fruits and berries were eaten fresh from the tree, cooked in stew, or dried in the sun and stored in baskets, pottery jars, leather pouches, and wooden boxes. Southwest Pueblo apartment houses had special rooms for storing grains, beans, piñon nuts, and meat. Lids were fitted onto storage containers to keep mice and other small animals from eating the grains.

Trade

Early Native Americans sometimes made use of outdoor markets where food was traded for other goods, or vice versa. Just as culture developed when a surplus food supply made time available to pursue the arts and sciences, so, too, an abundant food supply made trade possible.

Foods of the California Coast

There were many animals to hunt along the California coast. Rabbits, ducks, fish (such as the salmon), and mud hens were caught in small traps. Seeds, roots, berries, and tubers were gathered in large, flat baskets. Acorns were gathered from seven different types of oak trees. They provided the main diet of the Pomo and Maidu. The acorns were crushed on a stone mortar and then leeched with water to remove the bitter taste. Acorn flour was used for making breads and soup.

Foods of the Pacific Northwest

Hunting of sea mammals and land mammals was the main source of food for the Pacific Northwest cultures. Seals, halibut, salmon, and whales were hunted from small wooden boats. Fishing hooks and harpoons were made from bone and ivory. Fishing nets were woven from strips of sinew. Land mammals such as reindeer, moose, and bear were hunted with bow and arrow, spears, and clubs. Pointed boat paddles were used as weapons during sea mammal hunts.

Foods of the Arctic and Far North

In the Arctic tundra, meat from land and sea mammals made up the entire diet of the People during the winter months. A limited amount of edible plants and fruits was available. The harsh climate made agriculture impossible. Fish, beavers, seals, walrus, and sea lions were hunted from small, sealskin-covered boats in the summer months. In the winter months, ice fishing was practiced by cutting a hole through the ice and waiting for a seal to appear. The seal was speared when it surfaced for air. Seal and whale blubber provided fuel for lighting, cooking, and heating.

Polar bears, reindeer (Arctic caribou), and Arctic foxes were hunted from dogsleds and by foot. Meat was eaten raw or after it was cooked over an open fire or in a stew. Fish and meat were stored in leather pouches for the long winter months when hunting was difficult.

Foods of the Southwest

The Southwest pueblo cultures practiced agriculture on a large scale. The most important plant was maize (corn), which was introduced by the people of Mesoamerica. Maize was viewed as a sacred plant which was a gift from the legendary Corn Maiden. Maize pollen was used for healing ceremonies and for ceremonial sand paintings. Squash, beans, and maize were called "the three sisters" and were often planted together.

Melons, chili peppers, and fruit trees were also cultivated. Vegetables and fruits were dried in the sun and stored in the pueblo buildings. Turkeys were kept for their feathers and as a food source. The fruits of the saguaro cactus and the piñon nut were favorite treats.

Of note is the system of irrigation once used, quite sophisticated and successful. Irrigation was practiced in many areas, and some of these ancient irrigation paths still exist today.

Foods of the Great Plains

The most important food in the Great Plains was the buffalo, which once roamed across the plains in huge herds. Buffalo were hunted first on foot and later on horseback, following the introduction of horses into North America by the Spanish in the 15th century. The buffalo provided meat to eat, skins for tepee coverings, clothing, and bedding. Bones and horns were made into needles, paintbrushes, utensils, and tools.

Deer were also hunted, and pemmican was a common food. Birds were hunted for their flesh and for their feathers, which were used for decorations, dance fans, and ceremonial clothing.

Quest for Food (cont.)

Foods of the Woodlands

The People of the Northeast and Southeast Woodlands depended upon deer for meat. The antlers, hooves, and bones were used for tools, decorations, and household utensils. Bear, moose, duck, geese, wild turkey, partridge, quail, and other birds were hunted for their flesh, eggs, and feathers. The lakes and rivers were full of fish. Agriculture was also practiced. Corn, squash, beans, melons, and apple trees were grown in fields. Crops of the Southeast Woodlands included sweet potatoes, pumpkins, fruits, and berries. Sunflower seeds, berries, nuts, and tender leaves and ferns were mixed into stews and cooked in outdoor kitchens in the warm weather. In the cold season, cooking was often done indoors.

North American Trees

Native Americans believed that trees were kind beings who provided fruits, nuts, and berries for people to eat. Trees such as elm and cedar also offered bark fibers for textile weaving. Trees gave wood for cooking and heating as well as beams for building homes and lodges.

How many of the following trees can the students identify? Leaves, nuts, bark, and twigs may be brought into the classroom where and when available. Nature picture books can be used for a tree identification study.

Hardwoods	Softwoods
ash	cedar
basswood	Douglas fir
beech	hemlock
birch	larch
cherry	pine
gum	redwood
hackberry	sequoia
hickory pecan	Southern cyprus
magnolia	spruce
maple	
oak	
persimmon	
poplar	
red alder	
tupelo	
walnut	

Topics for Discussion

Review the importance of a balanced ecological habitat for plants, animals, and humans. Then, use some or all of the following questions for discussion topics.

1. What foods can you name?
2. What are your favorite foods?
3. What is your favorite recipe? How is it prepared?
4. Do all animals and people eat food? Why?
5. Do all persons around the world eat the same foods?
6. What are the factors which determine the food supply of each area?
7. Where do the foods that you eat come from?
8. Who grows and/or prepares the foods that you eat?
9. Which foods that you enjoy are grown in a field?
10. What kinds of foods did the Native Americans eat?

    (fish, buffalo, deer, fruit, vegetables, nuts, berries, roots, etc.)
11. Did the early Native Americans have supermarkets?

    (no)
12. Did the early Native Americans have outdoor markets where food was traded for other goods?

    (yes)
13. Have you ever picked fruit from a tree or garden? Whose garden was it?
14. What is your favorite tree? Why are trees important to us?
15. Have you ever cooked outdoors?
16. Does the food taste different when it is cooked over an open fire than when it is cooked on an indoor electric or gas stove?
17. How did the Native Americans start fires?

    (flint sparks or friction from rubbing two sticks together)
18. How did the Native Americans carry fire from one camp to another?

    (hot coals carried in clam shells and other containers)
19. How did the Native Americans store their food?

    (in jars, baskets, wooden boxes, parfleche pouches, etc.)

Parfleche

Directions: Color and cut out the parfleche pattern. Fold as shown. Tie shut with a piece of yarn.

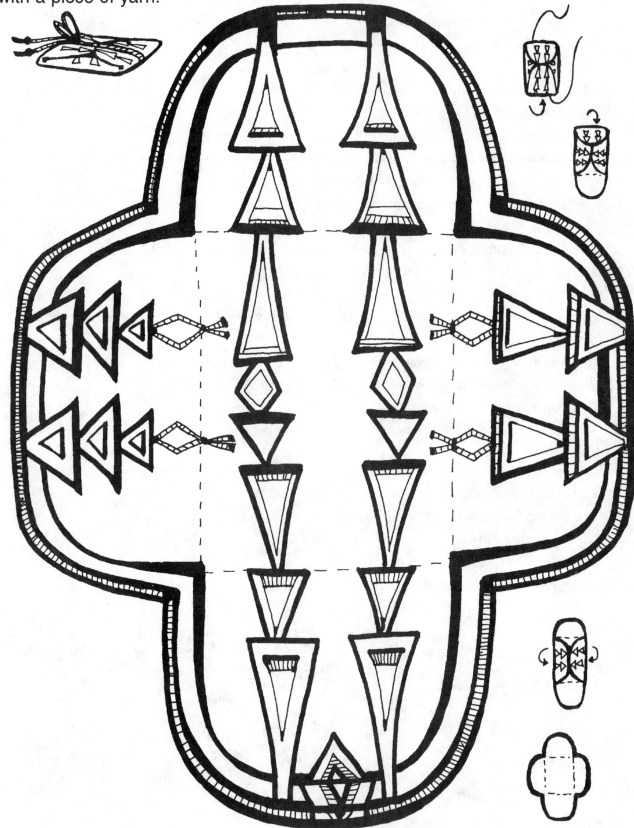

Name _____

Vegetable Stew

Directions: Name the vegetables in the stew. Then, count each kind of vegetable and write the correct number below. Color the picture.

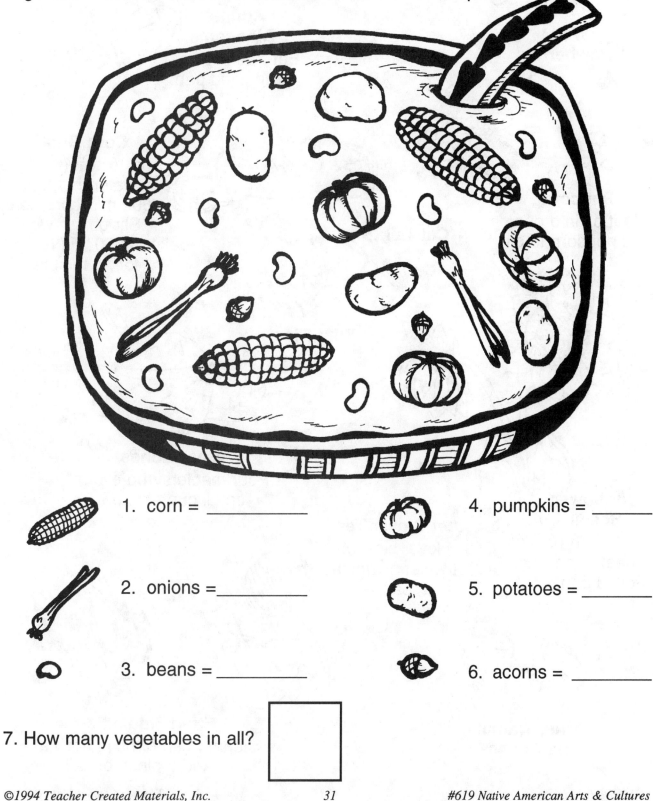

1. corn = _____

2. onions = _____

3. beans = _____

4. pumpkins = _____

5. potatoes = _____

6. acorns = _____

7. How many vegetables in all?

Traditional Foods and Recipes

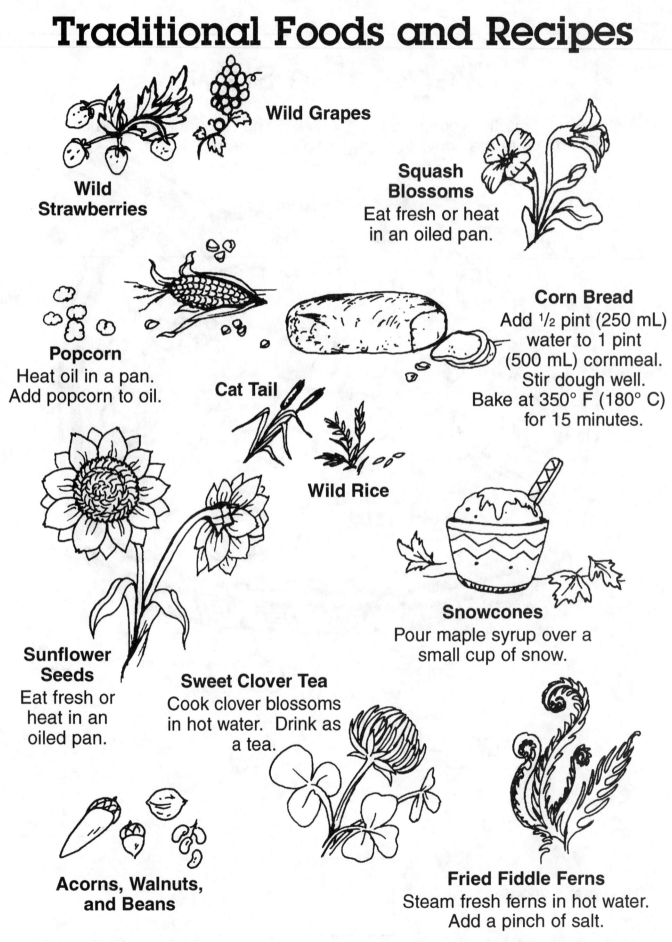

Wild Grapes

Wild Strawberries

Squash Blossoms
Eat fresh or heat in an oiled pan.

Popcorn
Heat oil in a pan. Add popcorn to oil.

Cat Tail

Corn Bread
Add ½ pint (250 mL) water to 1 pint (500 mL) cornmeal. Stir dough well. Bake at 350° F (180° C) for 15 minutes.

Wild Rice

Snowcones
Pour maple syrup over a small cup of snow.

Sunflower Seeds
Eat fresh or heat in an oiled pan.

Sweet Clover Tea
Cook clover blossoms in hot water. Drink as a tea.

Acorns, Walnuts, and Beans

Fried Fiddle Ferns
Steam fresh ferns in hot water. Add a pinch of salt.

Medicine Bag

Decorated leather bags were used to carry medicinal roots, berries, flowers, and plants.

Directions: Color and cut out the bag and handle. Glue the sides of the bag together. Glue on the handle. Add feathers or yarn fringe for decoration.

Name _____

Colored Maize

Maize is another name for corn. It grows in many colors.

Directions: Count how many ears of maize are growing on each stalk, and then follow the color code to color each plant.

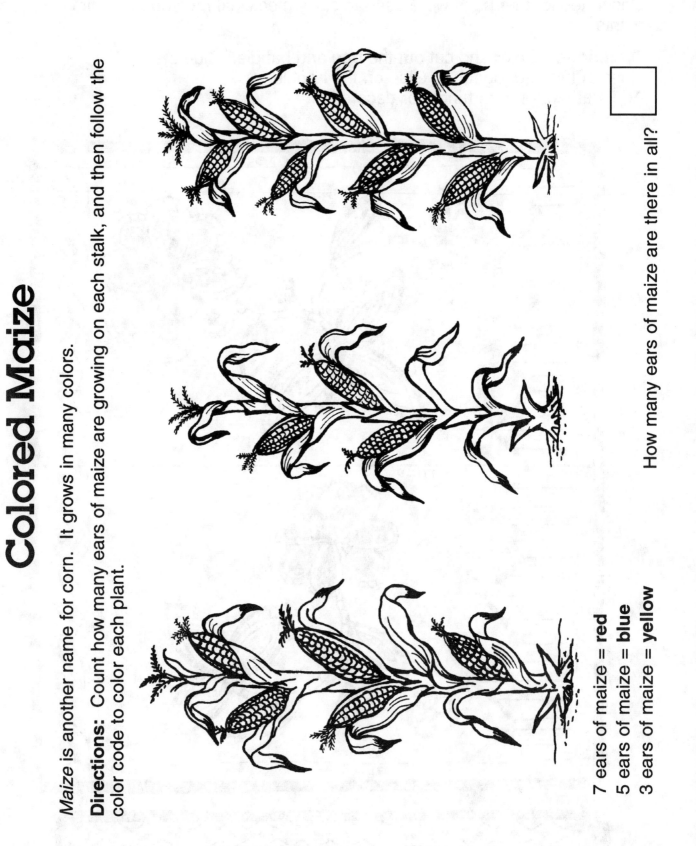

How many ears of maize are there in all?

7 ears of maize = **red**
5 ears of maize = **blue**
3 ears of maize = **yellow**

Name _____

Growing Maize

Maize is another name for corn. It was an important crop in the southwestern and eastern Woodland territories, and it was first cultivated in Mesoamerica thousands of years ago. To grow maize yourself, follow these directions. Then watch the corn grow.

Materials: corn kernels, moist potting soil, and self-sealing plastic bags

Directions:

1. Prepare a bag with soil. Fill the bag 1/3 full.

2. Plant several maize kernels in the bag.

3. Water the maize kernels and place them in window light.

4. Observe your plants' growth. (Note: Within five days the first leaves will begin to emerge through the soil. Seedlings may be transplanted outdoors in warm weather.)

5. Predict the outcome of the growth.

6. Record your observations on the "Growth Chart." Use as many charts as you need in order to follow the complete growth process of the plant.

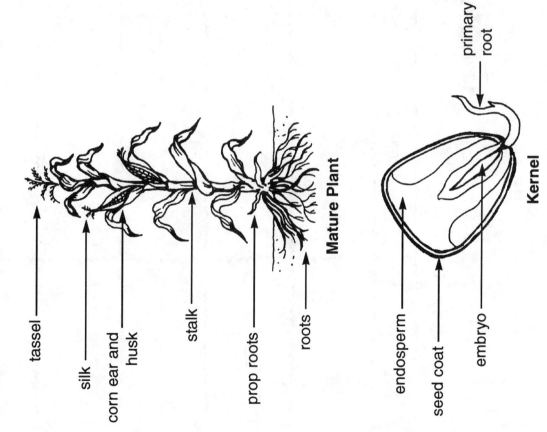

tassel

silk

corn ear and husk

stalk

prop roots

roots

Mature Plant

endosperm

seed coat

embryo

primary root

Kernel

Growth Chart

Name _____

Draw what you see each day.

Write your observations.

Day ____

Day ____

Day ____

Day ____

Day ____

Day ____

Name _____

Utensils for Cooking

Directions: Draw a line from each item name to the matching picture. Color the picture.

mortar and pestle

mixing bowl

cooking pot

eating bowl

corn grinding stone
   (metate)

food mat

Name _____

Draw Your Favorite Meal

Directions: Draw your favorite meal. Then, on the lines below, explain how it is prepared.

_____

_____

_____

_____

_____

_____

_____

_____

_____

Owl Box

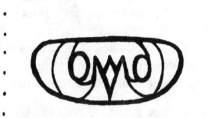

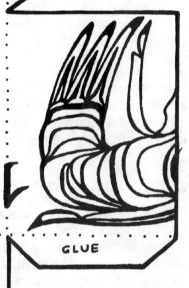

The Haida people from the Northwest Coast carved and painted boxes made from cedar trees. Food was stored in these boxes.

Directions: Color and cut out the owl box pattern. Fold and glue it where indicated.

Animals in Life and Legend

Notes for the Teacher

Animals are part of our everyday world. Children demonstrate a natural curiosity about animals. They enjoy playing with small creatures such as dogs, cats, and rabbits, and some children are familiar with larger animals such as horses and cows. In modern society, popular expressions compare animal attributes to human behavior. For example, we say that people are sly as a fox, scared as a chicken, proud as a peacock, strong as a bull, or shy as a deer. Children are delighted to imitate the flapping wings of a bird, the howling of a desert coyote, or the romping of a galloping horse. These expressions and activities reveal a direct empathy between humans and animals.

In order to familiarize students with animals, some classrooms keep pets such as gerbils, fish, or rabbits. Local nature centers may offer educational presentations about wildlife and natural habitats. A nature walk may be taken during which time the students observe, sketch, and take notations on the animals they see or hear. Bird and insect watching charts may be made and used as a focus for several group outings or as individual homework. Field trips to petting zoos, county fairs, or farms may also give the students direct experience with animals.

However one approaches the study of animals, it is an important and natural part of the school experience. In the bigger picture, many people believe that by understanding animal behavior, one can better understand human behavior. These individuals believe that we all share common ancestry with animals, or at the very least, we are all part of the same balance and harmony in nature.

Background Information

Animals played a central role in the lives of the earliest Americans. They provided meat to eat, furs for clothing and bedding, and hides for shelter and carrying bags. The bones, teeth, antlers, feathers, and claws of animals were used for tools, weapons, jewelry, and as ceremonial objects.

To discover which animals are indigenous to which areas, see pages 69-74. In order to challenge the students, remove the titles from the animal pages before duplicating them. Have the students match the animals to their appropriate habitats.

The Great Spirit

Native Americans have traditionally believed in a powerful life force which pervades all living beings, plants, and stones. This life force is known as the "Great Spirit," and it is called by many sacred names. Prayers, poems, and beautiful art objects are still made to please and invoke the blessings and wisdom of the Great Spirit.

Animals in Life and Legend (cont.)

The Great Spirit (cont.)

Traditionally, animals were revered as guides and protectors for humans. Because animals were living on the earth long before human beings, they were seen as closer to the great mysteries of nature. They were considered to be kind messengers between the People and the Great Spirit. The decorative and sacred visual arts of painting, etching, and sculpture depicted animals in both abstract and naturalistic manners, with loving attention and appreciation for the role which each animal played in the physical and spiritual well-being of the People.

Animals often appeared in dreams or in waking visions of children, women, and men at any stage of their lives. When a particular animal such as a bear or an eagle was seen in a dream, that animal was thereafter viewed as the totem (spirit helper) of the dreamer. Animals appearing in dreams were also painted on tepees, blankets, leather shields, and murals.

Clans across North America possessed special animal totems which were used as symbols of the clan name. Wooden totem poles carved by the People of the northwest coast depicted abstract animal and human faces and bodies.

Ceremonial dancers often disguised themselves as animals. For example, the Southwest kachina eagle dancers wore large eagle masks over their faces and heads and feathered wings over their arms. Transformation from animal to human and vice versa was a common theme in ceremonial dance and origin explanations. The elaborate animal to human transformation masks of the Arctic peoples were made from painted wood, feathers, animal skins, claws, fur, and antlers. These masks were hinged with movable parts.

Totem Poles of the Northwest Cultures

The People of the Northwest Coast carve totem poles today as they have for many generations. The tall cedar trees which grow in large forests provide wood for these poles. The trees are stripped of their bark and branches with a sharp axe. Then, they are carved and painted blue, black, and white. Totem poles may reach heights of one hundred feet (30 meters) or more.

The relief carvings on the poles depict abstract faces and bodies of animals and humans. The animals are symbolic of protecting spirit forces. Bears, beavers, owls, and ravens are carved one on top of another. Large, outstretched wings extend from the birds.

Totem poles are made for various purposes. A pole may communicate the clan name and personal animal protector (totem) of the family. Some totem poles commemorate special events or ceremonies. For example, mortuary poles for chiefs or other important people are carved on special occasions. Totem poles are also used as support beams in the architecture of homes and clan lodges. The Kwakiutl house posts, which are carved as totem poles, are such support beams. These house posts are traditionally believed to possess supernatural powers and can warn the family of approaching danger.

Some totem poles are carved on a giant scale while others are carved in miniature size. Regardless of their size, the abstract animal forms used in totem poles are graceful and imposing.

Animals in Life and Legend *(cont.)*

Fetish Animals of the Southwest Zuni People

The Zuni people of the Southwest are well known for their animal fetish carvings. These small animals may be carved from shell, coral, turquoise, jet, mother of pearl, clay, or sandstone. The miniature animals depict mythical creatures (such as the Thunderbird) as well as animals of this world (such as bears, eagles, or bison). Present-day Zuni artisans continue to create fetish carvings for sale and trade.

The earliest fetishes were found rocks that had the natural appearance of an animal such as a deer or a buffalo. Later fetishes were carved from sandstone, abalone shells, clay, or stones such as coral and turquoise. A stone fetish was formed by striking the stone with a hard rock and chipping away small pieces of stone. The finished animal was then smoothed with sand.

Arrowheads, feathers, and small stones were secured to the fetish with strips of rawhide. Tiny fetish animals were drilled and strung as necklaces and earrings.

An arrow leading from the mouth to the heart represents the life force, or the spirit breath, of the fetish. This heart line is shaped similarly to lightning or a snake.

The fetish animals were kept in a clay jar and ceremoniously "fed" crushed shell or turquoise. These fetish jars were carefully tended.

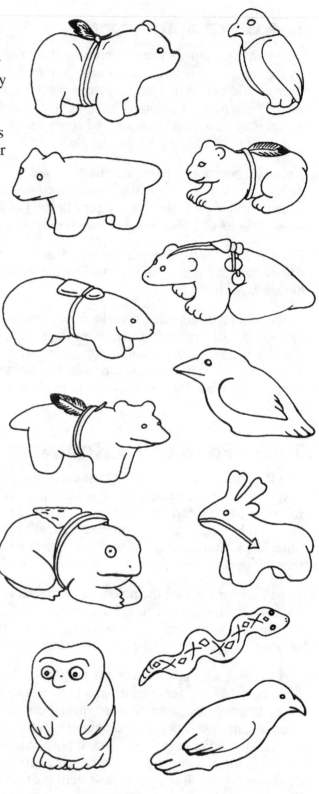

Celebration Day of the Fetishes

The winter solstice marked the observation of the *WE-ma-a-wa U-pu-k'ia*. This was the *Day of the Council of the Fetishes*. On this day, all fetish animals were taken from their jars and brought to the special altar. The fetishes were then offered food, incense, and prayers.

Animals in Life and Legend (cont.)

Categories of Fetishes

There are six different categories of fetishes in the Zuni religion. These are as follows:

1. **Masks, Clothing, and Ceremonial Objects:** used for ceremonial dances and rituals on special occasions.

2. **Ettone:** short reeds bound with cotton string into a round bundle for use in rainmaking ceremonies.

3. **Prayer Sticks:** wooden, arrow-like shafts with feathers fastened to one end, used to attract and please the spirits.

4. **Priesthood Fetishes:** small animal figurines, usually 3" to 12" (8 cm-30 cm) in length. The faces may depict both animal and human features.

5. **Concretion Fetishes:** found rocks which naturally resemble human organs, used to contact the spirits and to gain strength.

6. **Mili:** personal fetishes made of a perfect ear of corn ending in five symmetrical rows and kernels. These ears of corn were sometimes wrapped with feathers and used as prayer sticks representing the spirit of life-giving corn.

Priesthood Fetish Animals

The students can color and construct the minibook on pages 61-64 in order to learn more about some priesthood fetish animals. To do so, cut out each page of four, fold into a four-page book, and staple the 4 four-page books together to make a sixteen-page book.

Topics for Discussion

Assess background knowledge and initiate inquiry through question and answer sessions using the questions below. The responses of the students may be listed on the board or on a large chart if you would like.

1. What are animals?
2. Can you name some animals?
3. What can you tell me about these animals?
4. Where can we see animals?
5. How do we learn about animals?
6. What do animals do?
7. How do animals protect themselves from cold, heat, rain, etc.?
8. Where do animals live and what do their dwellings look like?
9. How are nests, burrows, caves, etc. prepared by animals?
10. What animals may have been present when the first Americans came to North America? (possibly giant sloths, mastodons, giant beavers, etc.)
11. What animals were important to the Native Americans in the past? Why?
    (Buffalo, antelope, dogs, horses, bears, birds, insects, rabbits, and more, were all important for two primary reasons. First, they provided food and other materials needed for living. Second, as part of creation they were important to the balance of nature.)
12. What role do animals play in our lives?
13. Are animals important? Can we live without them?
14. What animals have you seen in real life at home, in zoos, in preserves, in parks, or the wilderness?

Topics for Discussion *(cont.)*

15. Are there any wild animals around our school or in your neighborhood?

16. What wild animals lived here in the past?

17. What role did the animals play in the lives of the Native Americans?

    (Animals provided meat for food. They also provided fur and hide for clothing, bedding, and shelter as well as bones and other materials for the making of various tools and household/hunting utensils.)

18. What animals were important to the Native Americans in different parts of the country?

    (The following is a partial list:

    California Coast: deer, elk, moose, rabbits, ducks, fish, and mud hens

    Pacific Northwest: seals, halibut, salmon, whales, reindeer, moose, and bear

    Arctic and Far North: fish, beavers, seals, walrus, sea lions, whales, polar bears, reindeer [Arctic caribou], and Arctic foxes

    Southwest: turkeys and snakes

    Great Plains: buffalo, deer, and birds

    Woodlands: deer, bear, moose, fish, duck, geese, wild turkey, partridge, quail, and other birds)

19. Have you ever heard a legend (or fairy tale) about animals? What did the animals do in the story?

20. How are humans and animals alike? How are they different?

21. Do animals communicate with each other? How?

Haida Totem Pole

Pacific Northwest cultures carved totem poles of animals and human forms. This Haida totem pole depicts a raven and a beaver on top of a bear.

Directions: Color and cut out the totem pole, and then glue the sides together as shown.

glue here

glue here

46

Mystery Animal

Directions: Connect the dots to make the mystery animal appear. On the blank space, write the name of the animal that you find. Then, color your picture.

Name _____

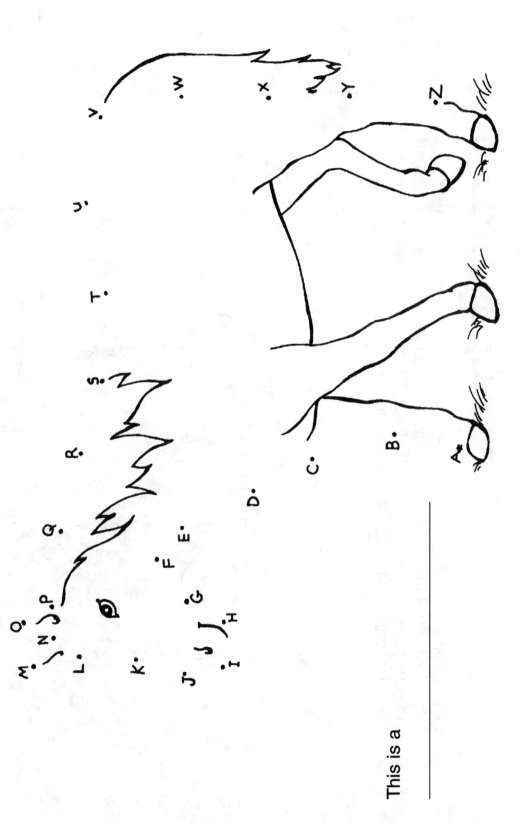

This is a _____

Stand-up Buffalo

Directions: Color and cut out the buffalo. Fold where indicated and the buffalo will stand up. Join your buffalo with the others of the class to make a small herd. (Or, each person in your class can make several buffalo. When joined together, you will get some idea of how large the roving buffalo herds once were.)

48

Name _____

Buffalo Herd

Directions: Draw a herd of buffalo following their leader. How many buffalo will be in your herd?

Grizzly Bear Puzzle

Directions: Cut the puzzle pieces on the dotted lines. Arrange them in their correct order. If you would like, you can glue them to another paper and then color the puzzle.

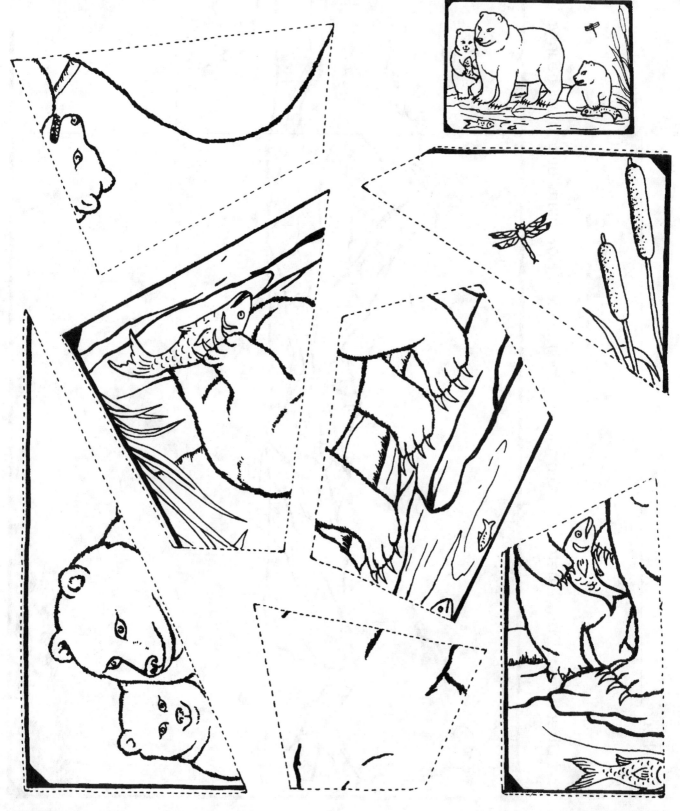

Name _____

Dot-to-Dot Elf Owl

Directions: To find who lives in the cactus, follow the numbers from 1 to 10.

Climbing Bear Cub

Why is the bear cub climbing the tree? Help the cub up and you will see!

Directions: Color the picture and the bear cub. Cut the cub and the tree trunk on the dotted lines. Move the cub up and down the tree as shown.

52

Flying Eagle Puppet

Directions: Color and cut out the eagle body and wings from this and the next two pages. Connect the wings to the eagle body with brads.

53

Flying Eagle Puppet *(cont.)*

Flying Eagle Puppet (cont.)

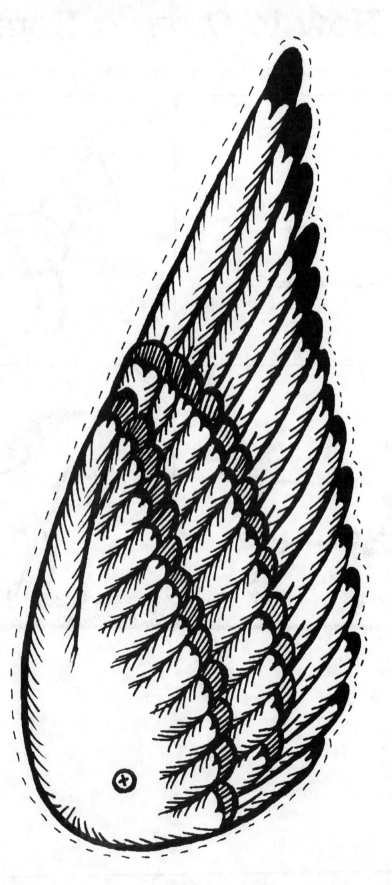

Name _____

How to Draw a Horse

Directions: Follow these four steps to draw a horse in the last box.

56

Name _____

A Bird's Eye View

Directions: Complete this picture to show what the eagle sees.

Name _____

Animal Shadows

Directions: Draw a line from each animal to the correct shadow.

Skagit Cedar Box Design

Directions: The Skagit people of the Pacific Northwest carved cedar boxes with animal motifs. To make a copy of a Skagit cedar box, color and cut out the raven, fish, and bear designs on this page. Glue the pictures onto a painted shoebox.

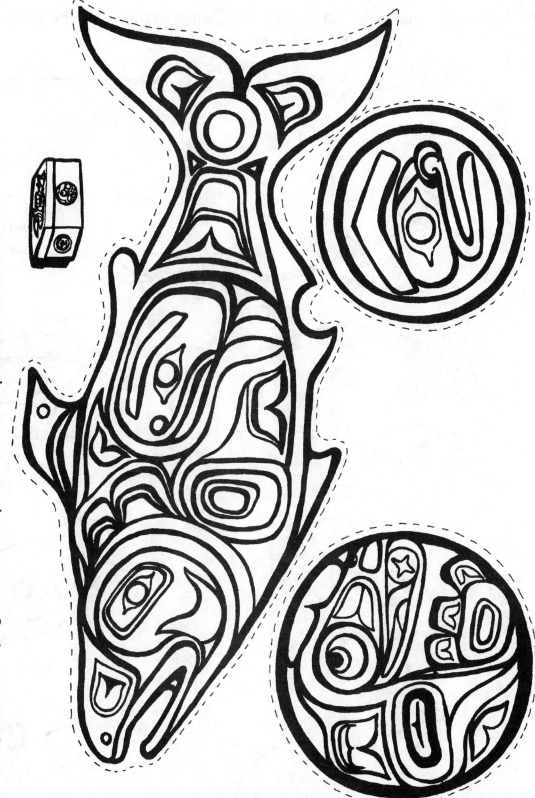

Zuni Animal Fetish Necklace

Directions: Color and cut out the Zuni fetish animals on the dotted lines. String them together on a piece of yarn to make a necklace.

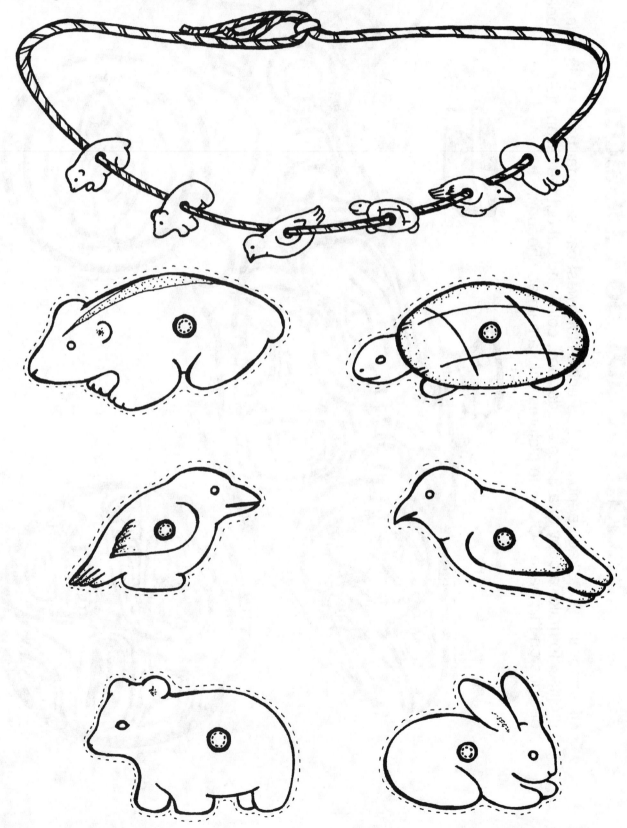

60

Fetish Minibook

(See page 43 for directions.)

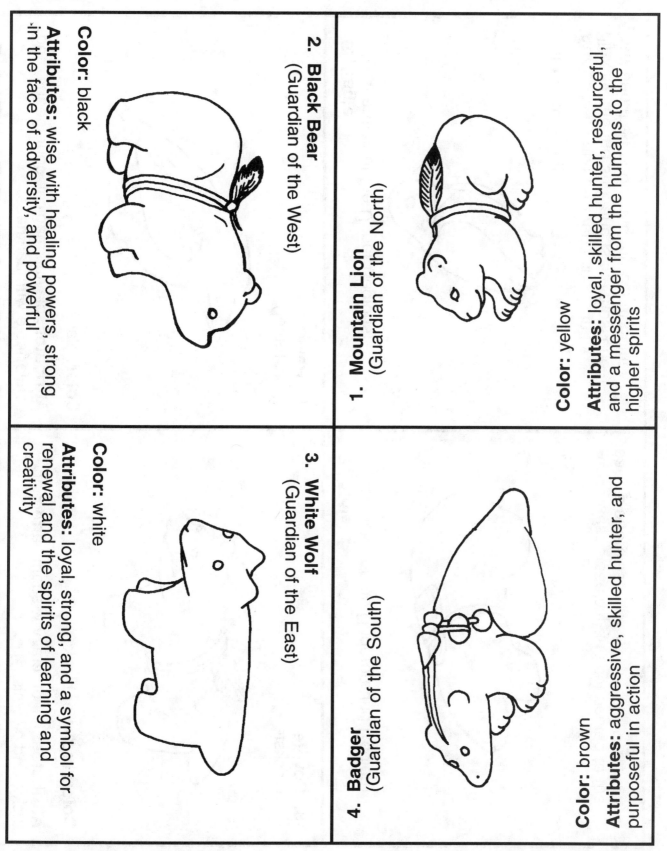

1. Mountain Lion
(Guardian of the North)

Color: yellow

Attributes: loyal, skilled hunter, resourceful, and a messenger from the humans to the higher spirits

2. Black Bear
(Guardian of the West)

Color: black

Attributes: wise with healing powers, strong in the face of adversity, and powerful

3. White Wolf
(Guardian of the East)

Color: white

Attributes: loyal, strong, and a symbol for renewal and the spirits of learning and creativity

4. Badger
(Guardian of the South)

Color: brown

Attributes: aggressive, skilled hunter, and purposeful in action

Fetish Minibook *(cont.)*

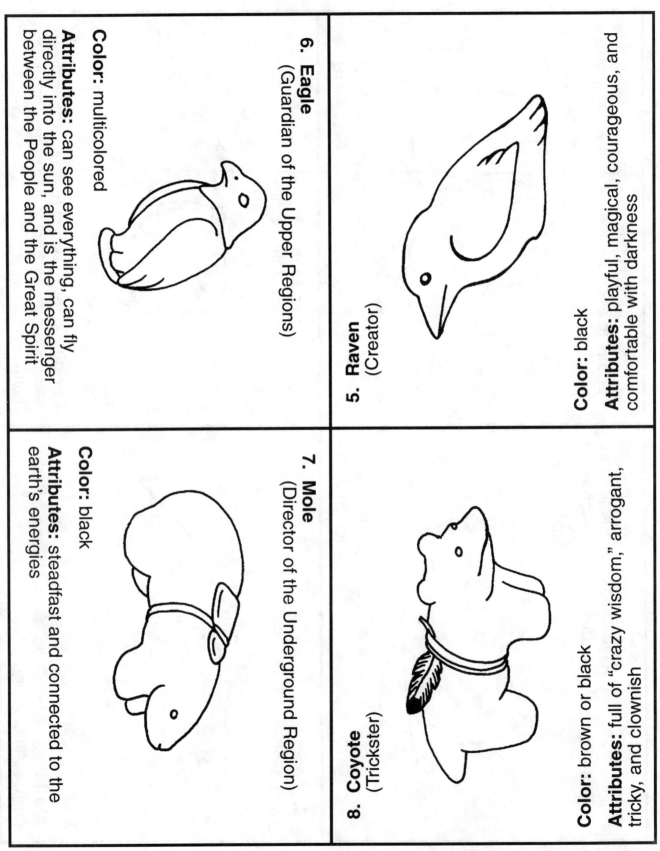

6. Eagle
(Guardian of the Upper Regions)

Color: multicolored

Attributes: can see everything, can fly directly into the sun, and is the messenger between the People and the Great Spirit

5. Raven
(Creator)

Color: black

Attributes: playful, magical, courageous, and comfortable with darkness

7. Mole
(Director of the Underground Region)

Color: black

Attributes: steadfast and connected to the earth's energies

8. Coyote
(Trickster)

Color: brown or black

Attributes: full of "crazy wisdom", arrogant, tricky, and clownish

Fetish Minibook (cont.)

9. Owl
(Communicator)

Color: brown

Attributes: has night vision and acts as the communicator between spiritual and physical realms

10. Rabbit
(Symbol of Illusion or Double Meaning)

Color: white or brown

Attributes: full of "crazy wisdom," tricky, lives by wits, and is a good guide

12. Turtle
(Symbol of the Planet Earth)

Color: green or brown

Attributes: non-violent defender and skilled navigator

11. Fox
(Trickster)

Color: red, brown, or white

Attributes: clever, sly, observant, loyal, and chameleon-like

Fetish Minibook (cont.)

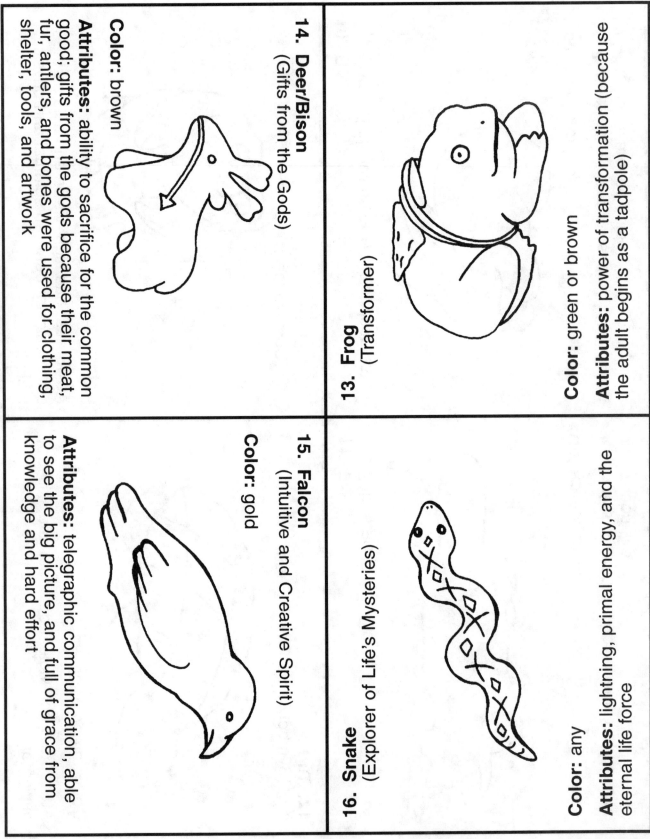

14. Deer/Bison
(Gifts from the Gods)

Color: brown

Attributes: ability to sacrifice for the common good; gifts from the gods because their meat, fur, antlers, and bones were used for clothing, shelter, tools, and artwork

13. Frog
(Transformer)

Color: green or brown

Attributes: power of transformation (because the adult begins as a tadpole)

15. Falcon
(Intuitive and Creative Spirit)

Color: gold

Attributes: telegraphic communication, able to see the big picture, and full of grace from knowledge and hard effort

16. Snake
(Explorer of Life's Mysteries)

Color: any

Attributes: lightning, primal energy, and the eternal life force

Animal Tracks Game

Each animal has unique tracks. Paw or hoof marks are left in the dirt as the animal walks. These form a trail which all Native American hunters learned to follow. This game will familiarize the players with the tracks of the bear, the deer, and the mountain lion. Up to three players can play at once. A single player can make predictions about how many turns it will take to get to the mountaintop.

Before playing, color, cut out, and fold the three playing pieces as shown. Also color the gameboard.

Have fun!

How to Play

1. Each player chooses a playing piece (bear, deer, or mountain lion).

2. Place all animal playing pieces at the starting line.

3. Arrange the game cards in a stack facedown.

4. Players take turns picking up a game card from the top of the stack. If the game card matches the player's animal tracks, the player moves his/her animal to the next square showing those tracks. If the game card does not match that player's animal tracks, the card is returned to the bottom of the stack.

5. The first player to reach the mountain wins.

Animal Tracks Game Cards

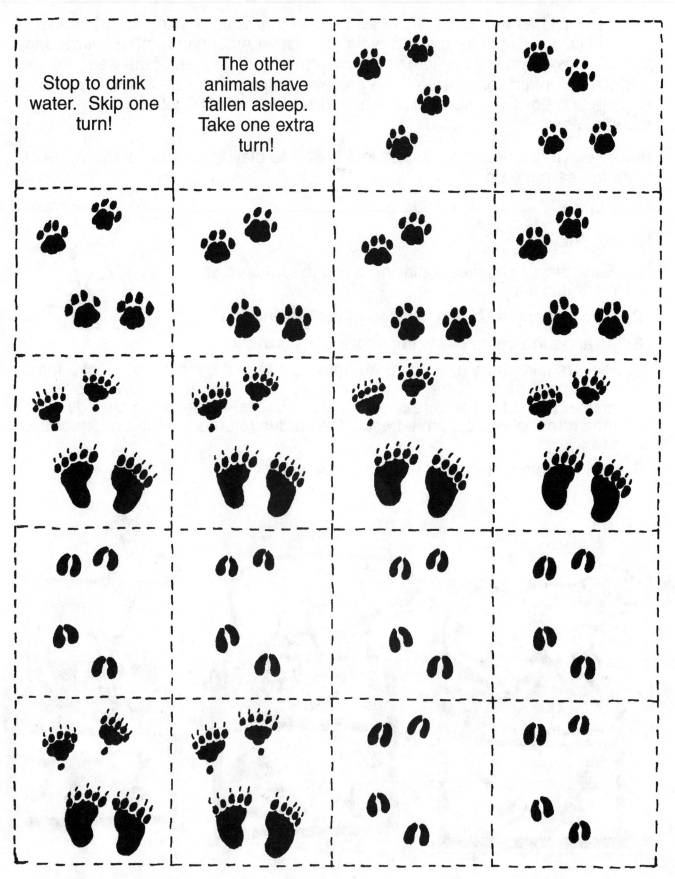

Stop to drink water. Skip one turn!

The other animals have fallen asleep. Take one extra turn!

Animal Tracks Game Board

Animal Tracks Game Board (cont.)

Start Here

Arctic Animals

Directions: Color the animals. Cut them out on the dotted lines and then paste them in their habitat.

fish

seal

walrus

snowy owl

Arctic fox

caribou

polar bear

lemming

ptarmigan bird

Arctic Habitat

70

Woodlands Animals

Directions: Color the animals. Cut them out on the dotted lines and then paste them in their habitat.

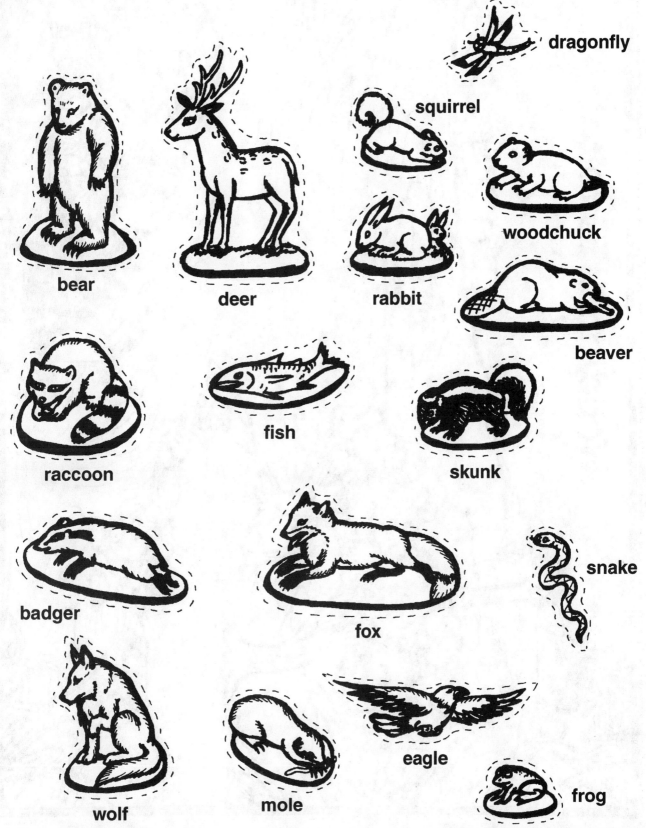

dragonfly

squirrel

bear

deer

rabbit

woodchuck

beaver

raccoon

fish

skunk

badger

fox

snake

wolf

mole

eagle

frog

Woodlands Habitat

72

Southwest Desert Animals

Directions: Color the animals. Cut them out on the dotted lines and then paste them in their habitat.

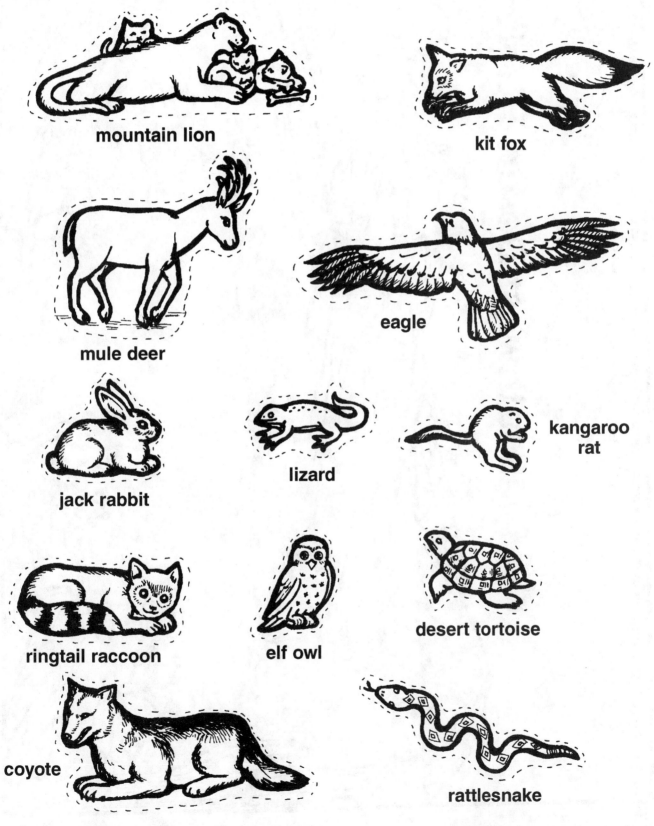

mountain lion

kit fox

mule deer

eagle

jack rabbit

lizard

kangaroo rat

ringtail raccoon

elf owl

desert tortoise

coyote

rattlesnake

Southwest Desert Habitat

74

Dance and Drama

General Background Information

Dance, music, and ritual drama have always played an important role in the cultures of North America. The major theme of all dance and drama is the importance of maintaining respect for the ancestral tradition of living in harmony with nature.

Therefore, the rain cycles, moon cycles, planting and harvesting dates, and the migrations of such animals as deer, bison, and coastal salmon were celebrated with days and nights of feasting, gift exchange, story telling, singing, prayers, dance, and music. Then the highlight of most village festivals came with the dance drama or prayer ritual.

These dance dramas served several functions within each community. They entertained, protected, and instructed the audience in methods of living in peace with other people, animals, plants, and the natural elements of fire, water, wind, and earth. By watching these dance dramas, young children learned the traditional folklore of their ancestors. The stories and histories performed by the dancers and singers involved the depiction of animals, ancestors, or messengers from the spirit world. The dancers were accompanied by many kinds of musical instruments such as drums of wood and animal skins, rattles made from hollow gourds, wooden flutes, and bells made from shells. The singers and dancers often wore makeup, masks, large head pieces, and colorful costumes. Dancers might carry objects such as musical instruments, feathers, corn, or painted shields. Women and men danced together in groups or as individual performers.

Many traditional dance dramas and rituals have endured unchanged for hundreds of years and continue to be performed today.

Dance and Drama (cont.)

Kachina Dancers of the Hopi and Zuni Cultures

Kachina dancers perform in the plazas of the Hopi and Zuni during the months of February, March, April, May, June, and July.

They represent the *Katsinam,* supernatural spirits who return to the earth each year to help people live a happy and prosperous life.

The Southwest mesa lands have very limited rainfall, less than twelve inches (30 cm) a year. Therefore, it is vital that the crops of corn, beans, and squash are planted according to the rain cycles. The kachina dancers come as guardians, protectors, and rain makers so that the crops will germinate and flourish. All kachina dances are related to the stages of farming such as planting, irrigation, harvesting, and storage of the prepared crops.

Kachinas are depicted as part human, part animal, and part mythical being. The kachina dancers may wear masks, costumes of many colors, and fancy headdresses with feathers, tree branches, or deer antlers attached. Some masks resemble birds, bears, butterflies, or even celestial objects such as the sun and the moon. Tall headdresses with repeating step patterns represent thunderclouds laden with precious rain. Others are adorned with bird wings, lightning rods, and animal skins. Kachina dancers carry such objects as eagle feathers, corn, rattles, tree branches, and bows and arrows.

Each kachina has special attributes and functions. There are over three hundred different kachinas. Children study these spirit helpers from an early age by watching their dances, listening to the prayer chants, and collecting small kachina dolls carved from wood and hung on the inner walls of their family homes.

The *Powamuyu* ceremony in February celebrates the end of the winter solstice and the hope for new life in the coming spring and summer months. The kachina spirits are welcomed into the villages at this time with gifts of food and offerings of woven baskets and painted pottery made by the women.

Dance and Drama (cont.)

The Kiva

Every pueblo village has at least one *kiva,* which is an underground ceremonial lodge with painted stone walls and an altar set near a fireplace. During the winter months, seeds are germinated inside the kiva, watered, and kept warm by fires. The tiny plants are then carried up a wooden ladder out of the kiva by the men and boys.

The kiva is a symbol of the *Sipaapu,* which, according to the Hopi, is the hole leading to the underworld from which the first humans emerged to the earth's surface long ago. The wooden ladder is the symbol of the pathway to the upper spiritual world where the Katsinam or Cloud People dwell. The kachina dancers prepare for the important public ceremonies for several months by living inside the kivas. Here they tend the seedlings, eat special foods, and pray for all of the people of their village so that they may be blessed with the guidance and protection of the kachina spirit messengers in the coming year.

The final ceremony takes place in July. This ceremony is called *Niman.* At this time, the crops have been grown and the people of the village all gather in the central plaza to bid the Katsinam farewell until the following year, when they will return once more from their traditional home in the San Francisco Mountains of the Southwest regions.

Kachina Dolls

The kachina dancers are given gifts by the village people as thanks for their help in maintaining balance and harmony between humans, animals, plants, and the natural forces of rain, sunshine, wind, and fire. The young boys are given small bows and arrows as symbols of the rainbow and lightning bolts which appear when it rains. The girls are given small wooden kachina dolls which have been carved by the kachina dancers during their stay in the kiva. These dolls are painted with bright colors and decorated with fur, feathers, twigs, stones, shells, and animal horns. Traditionally, the dolls have no arms and legs while other dolls are very lifelike, with human proportions. The Hopi are well known for their beautiful kachina dolls and dancers. They call their kachina dolls *tihu.* The colors of these dolls are associated with directions. Yellow represents the northwest, blue-green the southwest, red the southeast, black the zenith, and a mixture of these colors indicates the underground realm. A thin layer of white clay is applied to close the pores of the wood. The carved wooden figurines are then smoothed and painted with mineral and vegetable pigments.

Topics for Discussion

Discuss the roles dance, music, and drama play in your lives as well as the roles they played in the traditional cultures of North America. Audio and video recordings of Native American dancing and singing may be listened to and viewed by the class.

Use some or all of the following questions for discussion topics.

1. What is dance?
2. What is dramatic performance?
3. Do you ever dance? When and why do you dance?
4. What is your favorite kind of music? Why?
5. How does music make you feel?
6. Have you ever played an instrument? What kind?
7. Have you ever seen a live musical performance, dance, or dramatic play?
8. Have you ever worn a mask? When, where, and what kind of mask?
9. Does it make you feel like a different character when you wear a mask?
10. Do you like to sing? How does it make you feel to sing?
11. What kinds of music did the Native Americans of the past play?
    (primarily ceremonial and celebrational music)
12. What kinds of instruments were played by the Native Americans of the past?
    (rattles, bells, tom-toms, drums, flutes, etc.)
13. What kind of events were celebrated by dancing?
    (planting, harvesting, weddings, summer solstice, name giving, etc.)
14. What kind of singing was done by the Native American people of the past?
    (Often the songs told stories or were prayers.)

78

Name _____

Sun Kachina Dancer

"Taawakatsina"

Directions: Color and display the kachina dancer.

Name _____

Butterfly Kachina Dancer

"Polik Mana"

Directions: Color and display the kachina dancer.

80

Painted Dancing Shield

Dancers of the Woodlands and Southwest carried dancing shields of painted rawhide. The designs for the dancing shields were revealed in a dream.

back

Materials: paper plate, yarn, ribbons, feathers*, glue, paint, scissors, beads, and colored macaroni

Directions: Color a design on a paper plate. Glue feathers, yarn, ribbons, beads, and/or macaroni around the plate. Tape a handle to the back of the shield. Carry your shield and dance!

*Note: There is a feather pattern on page 85.

Rosette Patterns

Dancers of the Great Plains wore colorful rosettes for decoration. Traditionally, the rosette patterns are made with dyed porcupine quills.

Materials: glue, crayons, scissors, and paper (any color)

Directions: Color the rosettes on this page and design some of your own. Cut them out. Attach the rosettes to a paper strip to make a headband, armband, or legband.

Finger Puppets of the Arctic

Materials: scissors, crayons, and tape

Directions: Color the finger puppets and design some of your own. Cut them out and tape them to fit your fingers. Now, tell a story with the puppets and make them dance!

Dance Rattle

Rattles were made in many materials and styles. They were made from gourds, wood, bone, sea shells, turtle shells, and dried cacti. Beans or small stones were put inside the rattles to make sound. Across North America, dancers carried rattles to keep the rhythm as they danced.

Try making a dance rattle for yourself.

Materials: small milk carton, beans or pebbles, colored paper (or paint and paintbrush), craft stick, scissors, tape, glue, and ribbons, feathers, and beads

Directions: Put the beans or pebbles in the clean milk carton. Insert the craft stick into the carton opening and seal the carton and stick with tape. Decorate with paint or colored paper. If you would like, tie ribbons, feathers, and beads to your dance rattle.

Eagle Feather Dance Fan

Dancers across North America carried sacred eagle feather fans. To make your own version of the fan, follow these directions.

Materials: scissors, glue, and crayons

Directions: Color the feathers and fan handle. Glue the feathers to the handle.

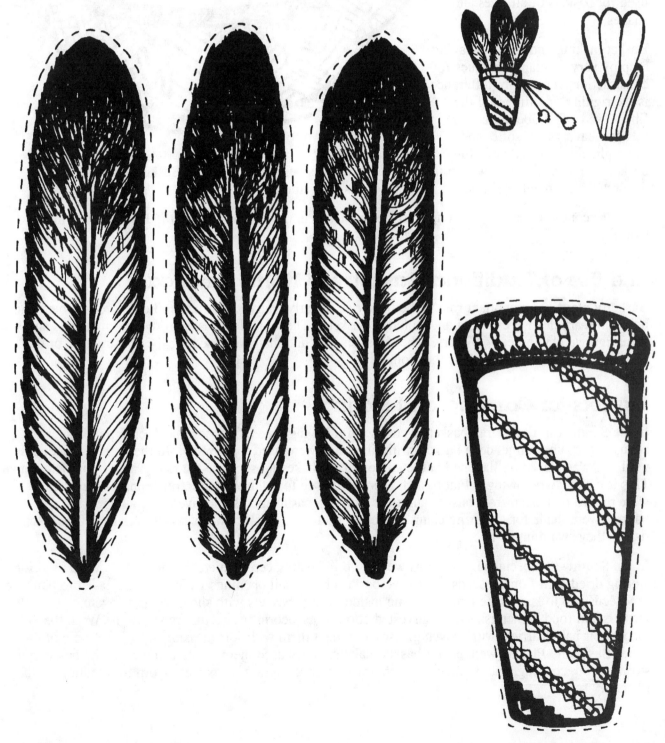

Basketry and Pottery

About Basketry

The word "basket" is an Old English word meaning a container made from vegetable fibers. All known cultures have produced baskets in some form. Local materials such as grasses, reeds, sticks, and bamboo have long been used for baskets of all sizes and shapes.

Basket making and textile weaving employ very similar techniques for construction. The major difference is the rigidity or stiffness of the fibers used. The fibers used for textile weavings are softer and more pliable than fibers used in basketry. Patterns can be woven into the basket as it is being constructed. Baskets can also be decorated with paint, embroidery, feathers, shells, and stones.

Basketry continues as an art among Native Americans in the Southwest and the Pacific Northwest Coast.

The Use of Traditional Basketry in North America

Basketry played an important role in the lifestyles of early Native Americans. Food, seeds, water, and household articles were carried and stored in baskets. They could be made from local materials and were lightweight and easy to carry. The sizes, shapes, and materials used for the construction of the baskets varied according to their function.

Baskets for Carrying and Storing

In the Southwest, flat or tray baskets were used for drying seeds, fish, cornmeal, chili peppers, and beans in the sun. Large, deep baskets with fitted lids were used for storage. In the eastern woodlands, wild rice was placed on flattened baskets in order to shake and separate the rice grains from their stems. This is called "winnowing." Flat baskets were also used to catch the nuts, fruits, and berries which were picked or shaken from bushes and trees. In the coastal shores and riverbank villages, special baskets were made for gathering clams and other shellfish. Baskets were also woven as nets to catch fish as they swam in the rivers.

In the Southwest, special basket drums were used in healing ceremonies. Some baskets were used for storing dried corn flour or seeds. The seed baskets had small openings which made it easier to pour the tiny seeds and to keep mice from climbing inside. Large baskets with shoulder straps were carried by farmers and food gatherers as they harvested corn, roots, acorns, or cactus fruits. In the West, the Pomo made their baby carriers with woven grasses and lined them with soft moss or fur. The People of the Great Basin and Plateau were expert basket makers. They used them for carrying food and possessions, storing food, cooking, and in trade. Woven grass capes and grass skirts were worn for clothing on the Plateau.

Basketry and Pottery *(cont.)*

Cooking Baskets

Special baskets were used for cooking. These baskets were woven very tightly and "tarred" on the inside with pine tree sap to make them waterproof. The cooking baskets were filled with water and meat and vegetables. Stones were then heated in a fire and placed in the basket. The hot stones made the water boil. The food was then cooked in the hot water. When the cooking stones cooled, new stones were taken from the fire and placed in the basket.

Basket-Making Materials

Baskets were woven from the fibers of local plants. Some of the plant fibers used were grass, bark, twigs, cactus, hemp, wood splints, and cane. Wicker baskets from willow or sumac branches were made in the Southwest. Baskets were also made from sedge grass, maidenhair fern, birchbark, elm bark, redbud, yucca, tule, reeds, mountain mahogany, cattail, sourgrass, and hazelnut. Palmetto leaves, straw, corn husks, and long pine needles are other natural materials once used in basket making. Basketry tools included needles and cutting blades of bone, stone, or wood. Yucca fibers, sinew, and grasses were used as sewing thread.

Making a Basket

Most baskets were made in two different ways: the coiling or the weaving method. In the coiling method, long strands of green grass were wrapped together to form a "rope." This rope was then coiled in a spiral pattern, working from the center outward. The coils were sewn together with grass or yucca fibers as the sides of the basket were built up.

The other method of making a basket was by weaving or twining plant fibers together. The basket weaver made a small base by crossing two rows of plant fibers and tying them together at the bottom of the basket. This formed the warp. The warps were then spread apart in a radiating pattern like the spokes of a wheel. Grasses or other plant fibers were then woven into the warp until the basket was the desired shape and size.

Basketry and Pottery *(cont.)*

Basket Decoration

Baskets were decorated with woven patterns of colored plant fibers. Some baskets were painted on the finished surface with brushes made from a chewed yucca leaf, rabbit fur, or the spongy leg bone of a buffalo. Paints were made from special plants and minerals which were crushed into a colored paste and mixed with animal fat. The paints were often mixed in shells or ceramic bowls.

Feathers, shells, and stones were also used to decorate baskets. Bands of geometric shapes were the most common designs, although animal and human figures were sometimes woven or painted onto the basket. The Navaho basket makers wove colored designs such as arrows, the sun, thunderbirds, and zig zag lines which symbolized lightning.

Birchbark Baskets

Birchbark baskets were made in the Eastern Woodlands. These were made from pieces of birchbark which were sewn together and pitched on the inside to become waterproof. Stencils of animals or leaves and flowers were cut into the bark, creating a design. These birchbark boxes were used for storage, carrying food and household items, and as "hot stone" cooking pots. Birchbark canoes were used to gather the wild rice that grew in the river water. Boxes and canoes of birchbark were admired for their beauty and strength, and they were a popular trade item.

Basketry and Pottery *(cont.)*

About Pottery

Since prehistoric times, clay from riverbeds has been used to make dishes, bowls, and statuary. Pottery shards have been discovered in the remains of ancient cities around the world. Pottery is made from soft clay which has been shaped and then placed in a fire pit or in a kiln to be baked or "fired." The firing process makes the clay piece brittle and waterproof. Pottery was practiced in the Southeast and Southwest regions of North America. Contemporary pueblo artisans have preserved the ancient pottery designs of their ancestors.

Traditional Pottery of the Native Americans

Pottery refers to clay pieces that have been heated in a fire or kiln (pottery oven). When the clay piece is heated (fired) in a kiln, it becomes hard and brittle. The fired clay may then be painted and used in many ways.

Because pottery is heavy and breaks easily, it was not a common item of trade. Nomadic groups did not carry pottery when they traveled. Instead, they used baskets or boxes for their storage and carrying needs. The people of the Southeast and Southwest made pottery dishes, plates, pipes, water bottles, cups, canteens, and animal or human figurines. Clay pots were used as cooking vessels in the Eastern Woodlands.

It is important to note that the Native Americans of times past only used natural, environmentally safe products for their artifacts. This is the special tie that all tribes had with nature and Mother Earth. The Native Americans were ecological caretakers of the earth, and the land benefitted from their expert use of it. The Native Americans did not pollute the earth as society does today with synthesized products.

The Use of Pottery in Daily Life

In the Southeast and the Southwest, pottery was used in many ways. Clay pots were used for carrying and storing food, seeds, and dried grains. Canteens and bottles of clay were used for carrying and storing water. Vases were also made from clay.

Both pottery and basketry were usually done by the women. Young girls would learn the arts of pottery and basketry by watching their mothers. The girls would practice by making miniature baskets and pots for their dolls.

The Zuni Pueblos created clay vessels in unusual shapes, such as a dish in the shape of a moccasin. Round bowls with handles were used to hold offerings of sacred corn meal in Zuni rituals. Square dishes were also made for serving food during the meal.

In the Southwest, pottery played an important role in daily life. When a person died, his or her favorite bowl was "killed" by making a hole in the bottom. This was done to free the person's spirit.

The Origin of Pottery

The Southwest legend of pottery's origins states that long ago, Old Clay Woman brought clay to each pueblo woman and taught her the secret of preparing and shaping it. She then showed the way to fire the pottery and to paint it with beautiful designs.

Basketry and Pottery *(cont.)*

The Anasazi Cliff Dwellers

The Anasazi lived over one thousand years ago in the Four Corners area of the Southwest (where Arizona, Colorado, Utah, and New Mexico meet). Their name is a Hopi word which means "the ancient ones." They are the ancestors of the present-day Pueblos.

The Anasazi practiced irrigation in their large corn fields. They created graceful black and white painted pottery and turquoise jewelry which has been found in their abandoned cliff dwellings. Modern Southwest pottery still uses the designs of the mysterious Anasazi.

Making a Coil Pot

Clay was gathered from the riverbeds and carried in a basket to the potter's home. The clay was cleaned and prepared by adding small pieces of old pottery to strengthen the new soft clay. Pots and jars were then made using the coil technique.

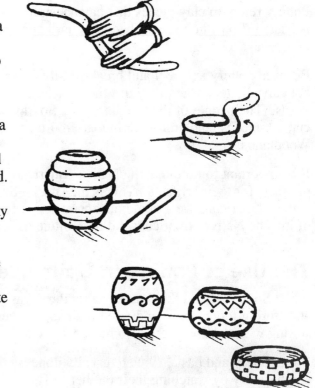

To make a coil pot, the soft clay was first rolled into a long "rope." Starting at the bottom of the pot, the clay was coiled in a spiral, and each layer was placed on top of the other. The pot was then shaped by hand. Tools of wood, stone, or bone were used for smoothing the sides of the pot. A thin mixture of clay and water, called "slip," was applied to the finished pot to smooth and polish the inside and outside surfaces. Fire pits or earthen kilns were used to bake the clay and to make it hard. The firing process took many hours to complete. A skilled potter could create a dozen clay pots in a single day and fire them the next day. When the pots broke, they were thrown away and replaced with new ones.

Decorating Pottery

Each artisan decorated her pottery in her own way. Traditional motifs were used for their beauty and their symbolism. Many of the pottery designs were originally used in basketry.

Clays were brown, white, yellow, green, or red, depending on the riverbed. Some pottery turned black when fired with ashes. The original color of the clay often changed after it was fired and painted.

In the Southeast, small tools were made to stamp designs on the soft clay. Most of the pottery of the Southwest was painted with natural dyes after it was fired. Painting was done with a softened yucca leaf. The most common design was repeating geometric shapes such as squares, triangles, arches, spirals, and dots. Human figures, birds, bats, deer, insects, and other animals and legendary spirits were also painted on the pottery. Designs were sometimes carved into the pot and then painted in a contrasting color. Turquoise stones or shell pieces could be used to decorate a bowl or pot. The rim of the pot could be round and smooth or cut into a zig zag pattern.

Modern potters often use traditional designs in new ways.

Topics for Discussion

Discuss the roles of basketry and pottery in early Native American cultures. Use some or all of the following questions for discussion topics.

1. What is a basket?

   (container made from woven plant fibers, bark, sticks, etc.)

2. What are baskets used for?

3. What kind of baskets can you think of?

4. For what purposes did early Native Americans use baskets?

   (storage, carrying objects, farming, gathering food, cooking, etc.)

5. What is pottery?

   (clay that has been formed into a shape and then fired in a kiln)

6. What do we use pottery for?

7. For what purposes did the early Native Americans use pottery?

   (art, cooking, and the transport and storage of water, seeds, food, etc.)

8. Have you ever seen any Native American pottery? How would you describe it?

9. Have you ever made a basket? What materials did you use? What did it look like? What did you carry in it?

10. Have you ever made a pot or a statue out of clay? What did it look like?

11. How do we usually carry our food?

12. How do we store water, milk, and juice?

13. How did the early Native Americans carry and store their food and water?

    (in baskets and clay vessels)

Birchbark Basket

Materials: scissors, crayons, and glue or tape

Directions: Color and cut out the pattern on the dotted line. Glue or tape the sides together as shown.

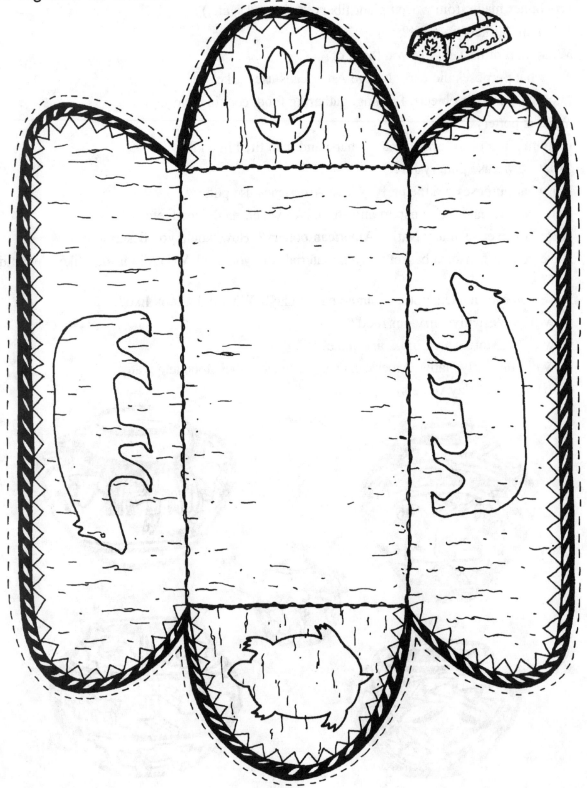

92

Corn Basket

In the Southwest, large cone-shaped baskets were used to carry corn from the fields. These baskets were made from woven yucca cactus leaves. Follow these directions to make your own paper basket.

Materials: 8" (20 cm) construction paper square, 12" x 1" (30 x 2.5 cm) construction paper strip, scissors, crayons, and glue or tape

Directions: Color a basket design on the square. Roll the square into a cone shape and glue or tape the sides together. Glue or tape the strip to the cone. (This will be the basket handle.) Color and cut out the corn and put it in your basket.

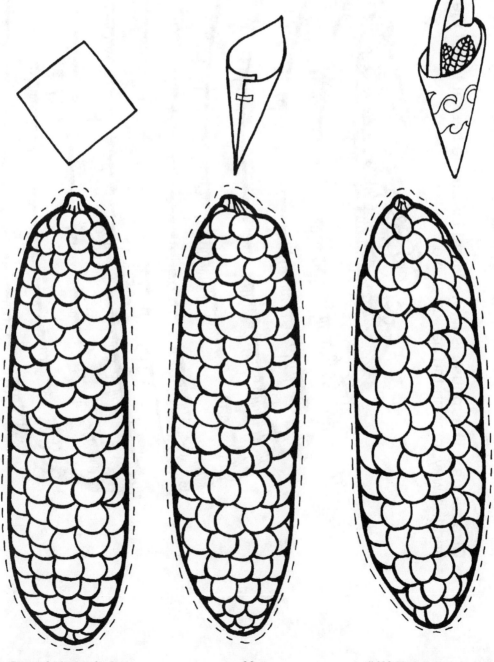

Basket Maze

Directions: The mouse is trying to get inside the basket to eat the corn. Help the mouse find the way through the basket maze.

Name _____

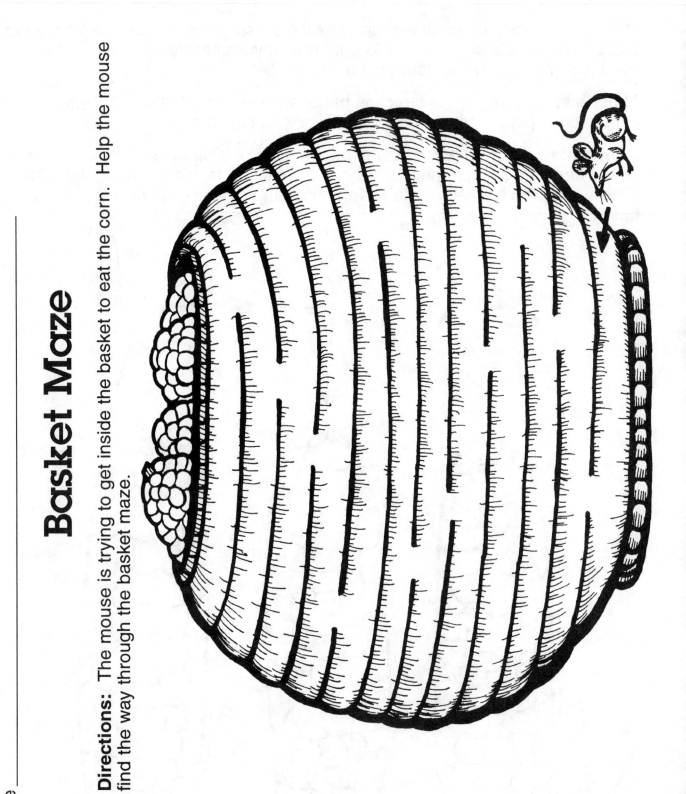

94

Coil Pot

Materials: soft clay, water, newspaper (to work on), and wooden clay modeling tools (optional)

Directions:

1. Form a small slab of clay for the base of your coil pot.

2. Take a large handful of moist clay and squeeze it into an oval shape.

3. Using both hands, roll the oval into a long coil. Repeat steps two and three several times.

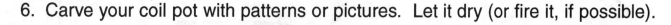

4. Attach the coils to the slab and press them together.

5. After the coils have been built as high from the base as you would like, smooth them together with a modeling tool or with your fingers.

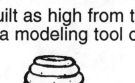

6. Carve your coil pot with patterns or pictures. Let it dry (or fire it, if possible).

7. Paint it when it is dry.

Origami Basket

Materials: thin paper, scissors, crayons, and tape

Directions: Cut from the paper a square of approximately 6" (15 cm) and a strip of approximately 8" x 1" (20 cm x 2.5 cm). Color a design on them. Fold the paper as shown. Tape the handle strip to the basket.

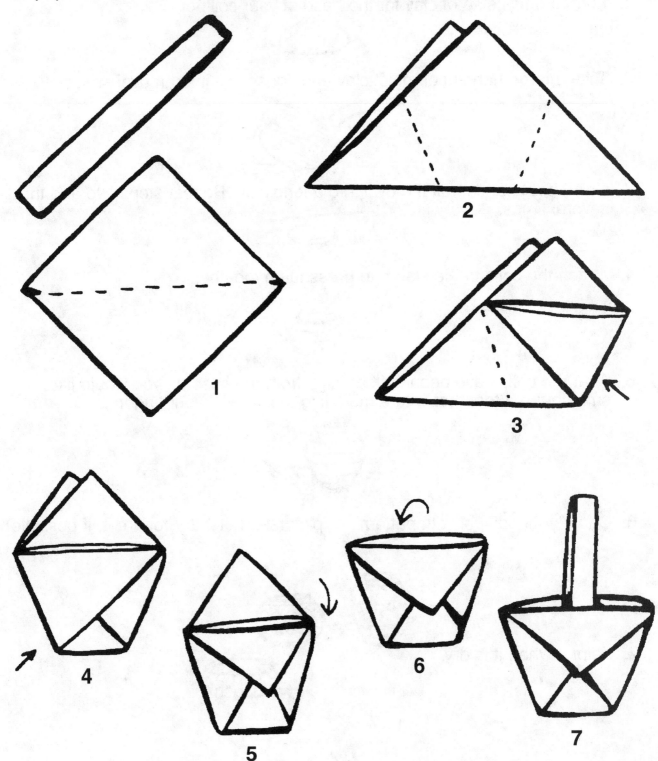

Colored Pot

Materials: paper, scissors, colored construction paper, and crayons

Directions: Fold the paper in half. Cut out this pattern and trace it against the fold. Cut out the outlined shape through both halves of the paper, and then unfold your paper. Color your pot.

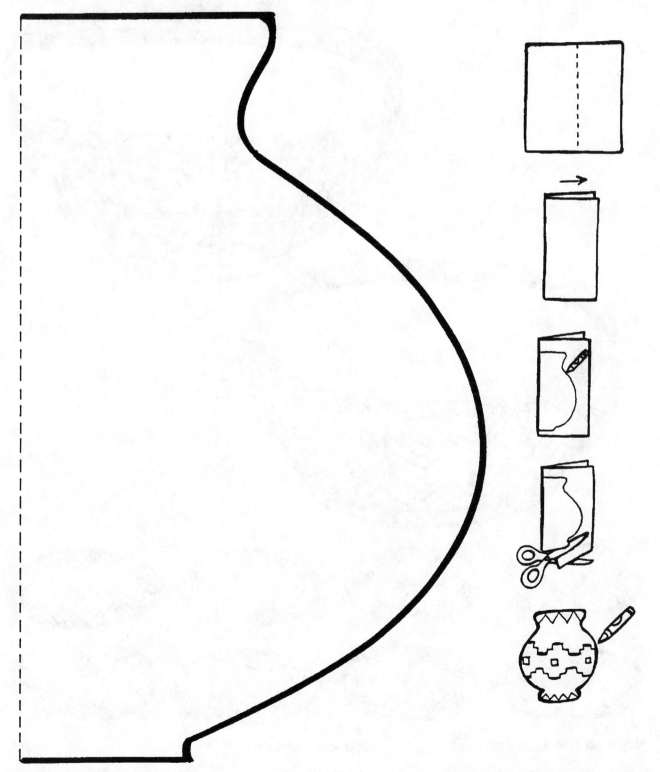

Name _____

Baskets of Yarn

Directions*: Help the weavers sort their yarn. Cut out the spindles of yarn below and paste them in the correct basket. Color the baskets when they are full of yarn.

*Note to the teacher: This is an open worksheet.

Name _____

What Is in the Basket?

Directions: Complete the picture by drawing something in the basket.

My basket is filled with _____.

"Pottery of the Southwest" Clip Art

Transportation and Trade

Travel Today and Yesterday

Early Native Americans traveled great distances for the purposes of hunting, trading, gathering together, and harvesting wild plants. Modern Americans travel for a variety of reasons as well, among them employment, school, vacations, and the visiting of friends and relatives. However, travel today is much simpler than it used to be. We take travel for granted. Unless the weather is very poor, motorized vehicles have made travel from home to school or to visit others a simple undertaking. When a family moves from one state to another, a large moving van comes to transport all of the household goods. Therefore, it is not necessary to limit the amount of personal possessions to what each person or a few animals can carry, as once was necessary.

Trade Today and Yesterday

Most Americans pay for food, clothing, homes, and household goods with currency. Credit cards make it possible to conduct business transactions with a number code, eliminating the need for currency. In earlier times, there was no standard currency as such.

Today we shop for food and clothing and other materials in a relatively impersonal manner. We eat food that was grown, harvested, and transported for sale by people whom we have never met. We do not know who knit the sweater we bought at a large department store. Sometimes we even may purchase an item that was made in a country we have never before heard about.

In contrast, the early Americans knew the source of all of the food, clothing, and materials which they acquired. Furthermore, everyone had an appreciation for the amount of labor and care that was required by the artisan in order to create a woven wool blanket, a ceramic pot, or a painted buffalo robe. In general, personal possessions were limited and treated with great care. Trade and barter were common practices. The trade fairs in North America brought many cultural groups together for the exchange of goods as well as for the enjoyment of dances and feasting celebrations.

Transportation and Trade *(cont.)*

The Need to Travel

The land area of North America covers over 7,000 square miles (11,000 km). Traversing the land, early Native Americans traveled long distances by land and water. Journeys were taken by single families, small bands, and large groups in order to follow the grazing herds of buffalo, reindeer, or deer. The harvesting of wild fruits, nuts, seeds, and berries was another reason to travel. Important events such as trade fairs and pow-wows brought the people of many areas together for the exchange of furs, beads, and foods. Permanent migrations sometimes occurred when a water supply ran low or when another clan moved into the area.

Travel by Land and Sea

Long journeys were taken by the Native Americans. These travels could take days, weeks, or even months. Travel was done in all seasons when necessary. The methods of transportation and the preparation for travel varied across the country. When the Native Americans traveled at night, they navigated by the stars. The star patterns or constellations helped the People know their direction of travel.

Winter Travel in the Arctic and Far North

The People of the Arctic and Far North crossed snowy land and frozen rivers by sleds which were pulled by a single person or by trained teams of huskies. These toboggans were also used to carry food and household goods across the snow. Young children and old or sick persons were also carried in this manner.

Wooden skis and snowshoes were worn in the snow. Snowshoes were made from wood and thin strips of sinew woven together by the women. These snowshoes kept the person from sinking in the deep, soft snow. Animals were sometimes tracked across the snow by hunters wearing such shoes. This made winter hunting somewhat difficult and sometimes dangerous.

Transportation and Trade (cont.)

Summer Travel in the Arctic and Far North

In the summer months, the Inuit and Aleut Peoples of the Far North and Arctic lands traveled by small sealskin boats such as the umiak and the kayak. These boats were guided by long, flat paddles and were used by one person. It required great skill to control these boats. If the boat turned upside down, it was necessary to turn upright quickly without falling out of the boat! Sea mammals and fish were hunted from these boats with harpoons and fishing hooks.

Travel in the Pacific Northwest and California

The Pacific Northwest Coast Peoples such as the Haida and the Tlinget traveled by foot for short distances. Large and small wooden boats or canoes with paddles were used along the ocean coast and on inland rivers. These boats were carved from hollowed cedar logs. The logs were stripped of their bark before they were hollowed by burning and carving with sharp tools. The wooden paddles and the sides of the boats were carved with bold designs. The carved designs were then painted with red, blue, black, and white paints. These boats carried up to sixty persons. Smaller boats were made for the use of individual families. Every coastal town had a busy harbor with many boats anchored along the shore.

Potlatch Feasts: Occasions to Travel

Potlatch celebrations were held by certain families in the permanent coastline towns in the Pacific Northwest. These were events of great importance for trade and the exchange of gifts. Feasting, storytelling, and dancing could last for several days. Entire families would travel by boat or overland to join in the Potlatch.

The People of the Pacific Northwest were wealthy. They had a steady supply of food from hunting and gathering. The artisans had the community support as well as the time to create woven blankets, carved totem poles, wooden masks, fishing and hunting tools, robes, and basketry. These items were highly valued and were traded widely.

Transportation and Trade *(cont.)*

California Coastal Towns

In California, plank boats were made from thin planks of wood. These planks were sewn together with sinew and caulked with asphalt for waterproofing. A large supply of seafood and wild plants such as acorns provided a comfortable lifestyle for the People of California. Heavy trade took place along the coast and farther inland. Sea shells were a valuable item of trade from California.

Travel in the Southwest and the Great Plains

The Southwest desert was traveled by foot, by small river boats, and by horse. Horses allowed great mobility to the Peoples of the Southwest and the Great Plains. For example, the Navaho could herd their sheep on horseback. The horse made it possible for the hunters of the Great Plains to follow the buffalo for long distances. This assured an adequate supply of food for the many Peoples of the Great Plains area. Horses were a sign of wealth and made life much easier. The strength and grace of the horse was celebrated in song, poetry, and art. Without horses, hunting by foot was difficult and travel was limited.

The Travois

Before the Spanish introduced horses into North America over four hundred years ago, household goods and food were carried by the dog travois. *Travois* (trah-VOY) is derived from the French language. It means "traverse." The travois were used to transport food and household goods. Each was made from two long poles with leather bands that held the carried goods. The poles were tied over the shoulders of the dog, and the animal dragged the travois across the Great Plains. Meat from a hunt or other goods were tied to the travois, and then the dog would drag the entire load over the mountain passes and throughout the valleys. Small tepees were rolled up and tied to the dog travois when the Plains People went on hunting trips. When the horse came to the Great Plains the travois became larger to fit the body of the horse. Now it was possible for the hunters to travel with large tepees and to carry hundreds of pounds of weight as they traveled with their horses.

Transportation and Trade (cont.)

Travel by Water

In the Great Plains and Southwest, small boats were used for travel down a large river, such as the Colorado River which runs through the Grand Canyon. Boats of reeds were made in the summer months. Bullboats were small tub-shaped boats made from animal skins stitched over a frame of bone or wood. Several people could ride in the bullboat, which was steered with a paddle. These boats were lightweight and could be lifted from the water and carried overland if necessary.

Travel in the Eastern Woodlands

The rivers were the highways of the Woodlands Peoples. The Missouri and Mississippi Rivers were very important routes for travel and trade. The birchbark canoe and the elm bark canoe were made in the Eastern Woodlands. These were not very heavy and could be carried on top of the head and shoulders when the river journey was over. The canoe was made by gluing large pieces of birchbark or elm bark to a frame of wooden poles. The bark pieces were then joined together and sealed with pine pitch. This would make the boat watertight. These canoes were a popular trade item. When the rivers became frozen in the winter months, sleds and snowshoes were used for travel across the snow and ice. Wooden skis were made from narrow planks of wood and strapped to the boots for cross country skiing.

Ancient Foot Trails and Modern Highways

Narrow foot trails criss-crossed the huge forests and mountain passes of North America. Wheeled wagons were not used by the early Native Americans when they traveled along these footpaths. The idea of the wheel was understood, but wheeled vehicles were not practical for traveling across the mountain passes and forest trails. Horses and dogs could easily follow these foot trails.

Many of the old trails have been smoothed and paved over for motor vehicles. Today, it is not legal to walk on the major highways across America.

Trade Goods

Trade routes were used for thousands of years. These trade routes were traveled in order to exchange goods and to share ideas. Special baskets, furs, jewelry, clothing, sculpture, medicines, tools, weapons, shells, eagle feathers, blankets, and masks were traded by the People of all areas. The Plains People traded beaver pelts and buffalo hides for porcupine quills from the Far North. The Zuni fetish sculptures of the Southwest were traded for shells and beads from the ocean coastlines. Quartz crystals and obsidian from the Rocky Mountains were traded for flint from southern Canada. Tobacco was traded everywhere it was not grown. Salt was traded in agricultural regions. Shells and woven baskets from the People of California were famous trade items.

Transportation and Trade *(cont.)*

Wampum Belts

Wampum is a word from the Algonquin language. The translation is "white beads." Wampum belts made from white and purple clam shells were used as items of trade and also as a kind of money in the eastern areas of North America. When treaties were made, the exchange of wampum belts was required.

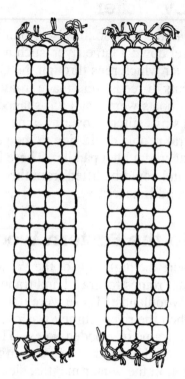

Special designs were woven into the wampum belts to relay messages. For example, if the design showed two people holding hands, it was a sign of friendship. When the wampum belt was red, it was a sign of fighting.

The People traded animal skins, woven blankets, and wampum belts in exchange for cloth, silk ribbons, glass beads, and metal tools and weapons from European countries.

Most wampum belts were about three feet (91 cm) long. Very few have been preserved.

Trade Centers and Travel Routes

There were several major trade routes and trading centers in North America. One such was the Mandan trading center on the banks of the Missouri River. Here lived professional, full-time traders who helped organize the trading activities of the many different people who came to trade. Mandan became a trade language. Sign language was used by the People when they met to trade with one another and did not share the same spoken language.

Trade Center Activities

Fighting was not allowed at important trading centers. A great exchange of ideas, oral storytelling, medicine knowledge, and dance took place at the trading centers. Everyone benefited from the trading practices across North America. Long journeys over land and water were taken in order to join in the activities at such centers. Mexican culture and trade goods were brought north by a vital trade route which ran along the eastern foothills of the Sierra Madre Mountains. The Mississippi River was also a "highway" for travel and trade from the Southeast Coast to the Midwest and Eastern Woodlands. In Mexico, chocolate beans were used as money. Precious gems and metals such as gold, silver, and copper were traded throughout North America.

Trade and Barter Game

The students might enjoy bringing several items from home or from the classroom to "trade" with one another. They might also try trading in sign language or in pictographs. Remind them that trading fairly means that both parties believe they have received objects of equal value.

Topics for Discussion

Discuss methods of transportation to which you are accustomed. Also discuss reasons for travel today. Then, review the contrasts between modern day shopping and traditional trade and barter in North America. (Make sure that the students understand that Native Americans today use the same methods of transportation and "trade" as does everyone else.)

Use some or all of the following questions for discussion topics.

1. Do you travel?
2. Where do you travel?
3. When you travel, what mode of transportation do you use?
4. Why do you travel?
5. What is your favorite kind of transportation?
6. Who carries your clothes and other possessions when you travel?
7. How much could you take along with you if you had to carry all of your possessions yourself when you traveled? How far could you carry them?
8. How did the early Native Americans travel?
   (by canoe, raft, horse, sled, on foot, etc.)
9. Why did the early Native Americans travel?
   (to trade, to hunt, to gather wild crops, etc.)
10. Which types of traditional travel are still practiced today?
    (walking, running, skiing, sledding, tobogganing, horseback riding, boating)
11. What did the early Native Americans use for money when they shopped?
    (shells, beads, furs, etc.)
12. What kind of goods did the early Native Americans trade?
    (furs, feathers, shells, food, beads, jewelry, etc.)
13. Could you invent a new way to travel and shop in the future?
14. If you were a trader, what would you trade?
15. Who would make your goods?
16. With whom would you trade?

Birchbark Canoe

The birchbark canoe was made from birchbark pieces glued onto a wooden frame. The People of the Eastern Woodlands traveled along the rivers and lakes in birchbark or elm canoes. Wooden paddles steered the canoe.

Follow these directions to make a model birchbark canoe.

Materials: scissors, crayons, and glue or tape

Directions: Color, cut, and glue or tape your canoe as shown.

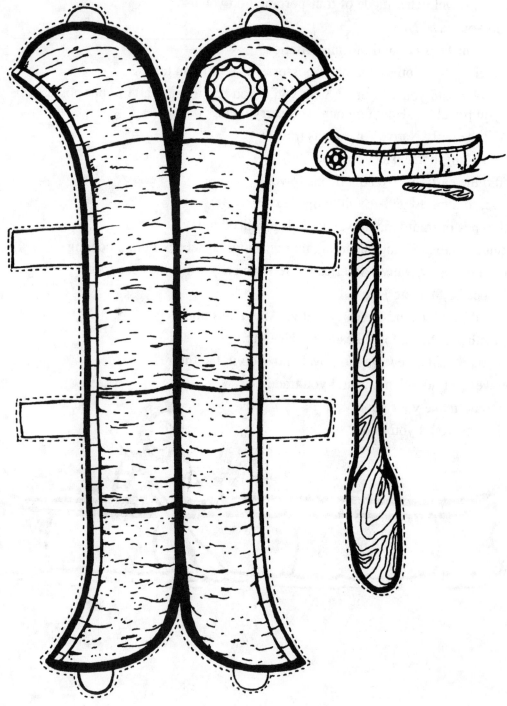

Haida Wooden Boat

The Haida made large boats of cedar and redwood trees. These boats were carved and painted in bold designs.

Follow these directions to make a model Haida boat.

Materials: scissors, crayons, and glue or tape

Directions: Color the boat and paddle and cut them out on the dotted lines. Tape the boat ends as shown.

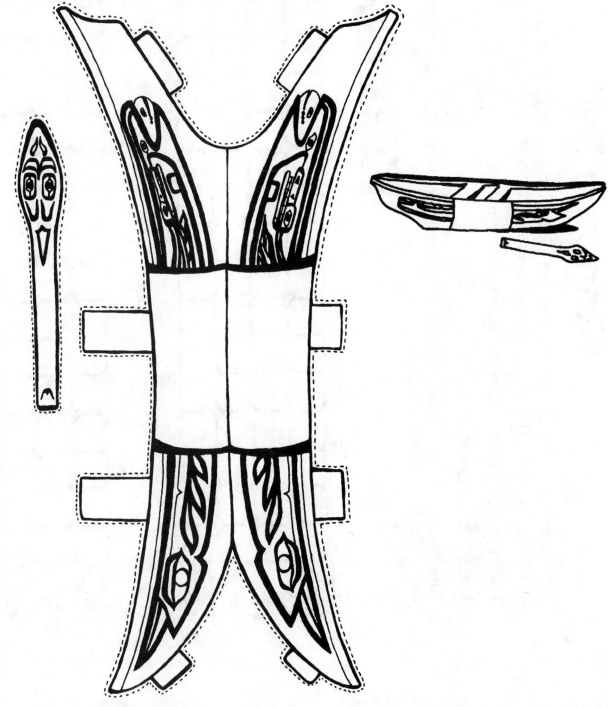

Wampum Belt

Wampum belts were used in the Eastern Woodlands as trade items and as records of treaties. The wampum belts were usually made from white and purple clamshells.

Follow these directions to make a model wampum belt.

Materials: scissors and crayons

Directions: Color a grid design on your wampum belts. Cut out the belts on the dotted lines. Trade one with a friend.

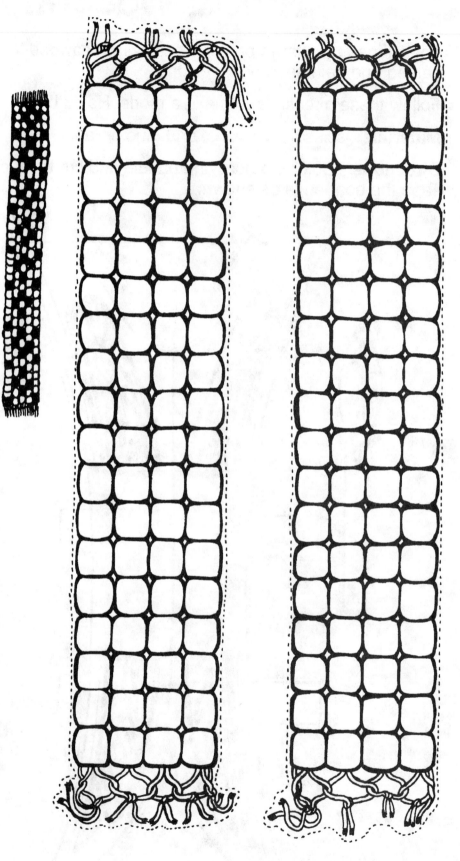

Name _____

Snowshoe Crossword Puzzle

Solve the puzzle to find out how early Native Americans traveled.

Directions: Match each word in the word bank to a picture clue. Fill in the puzzle blanks with the correct words.

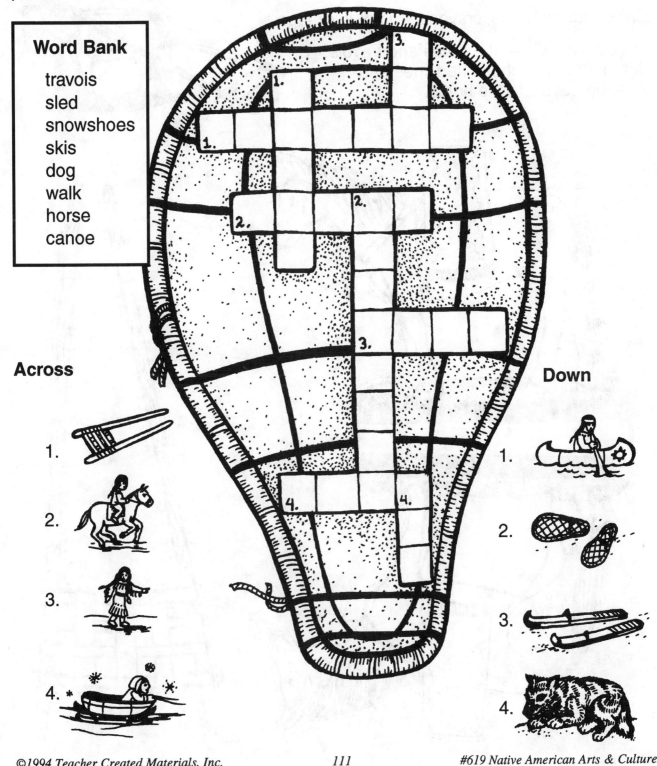

Word Bank

travois
sled
snowshoes
skis
dog
walk
horse
canoe

Across

1.

2.

3.

4.

Down

1.

2.

3.

4.

Horse Travois

The horse travois was made from two long wooden poles which were tied by leather straps. Horses could drag the travois along the ground to carry food, household goods, and small children. Folded tepees were also carried on the horse travois.

Follow these directions to make a model horse travois.

Materials: scissors, crayons, and glue or tape

Directions: Color the horse and travois. Cut them out on the dotted lines and tape the travois to the horse.

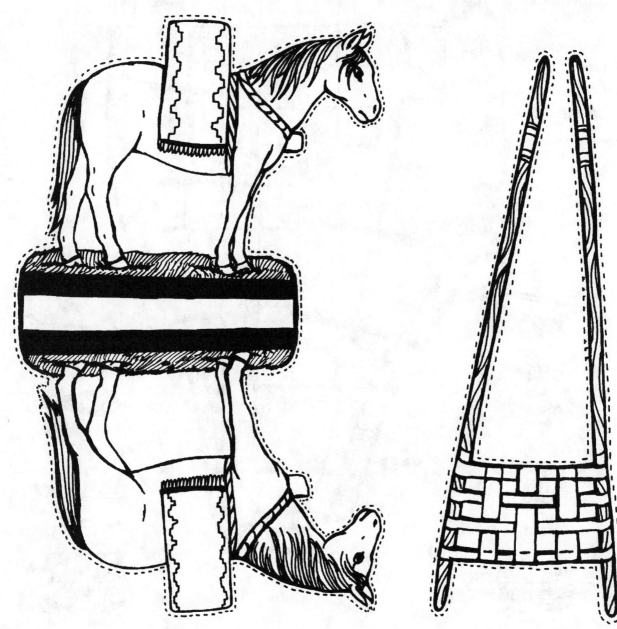

Canoe Race

Directions for the Teacher: Color and cut out the canoe playing pieces and fold the flap under each canoe. Color the gameboard, adding whatever review questions you would like. To play, have the students answer the questions. The first player to solve each problem wins the race.

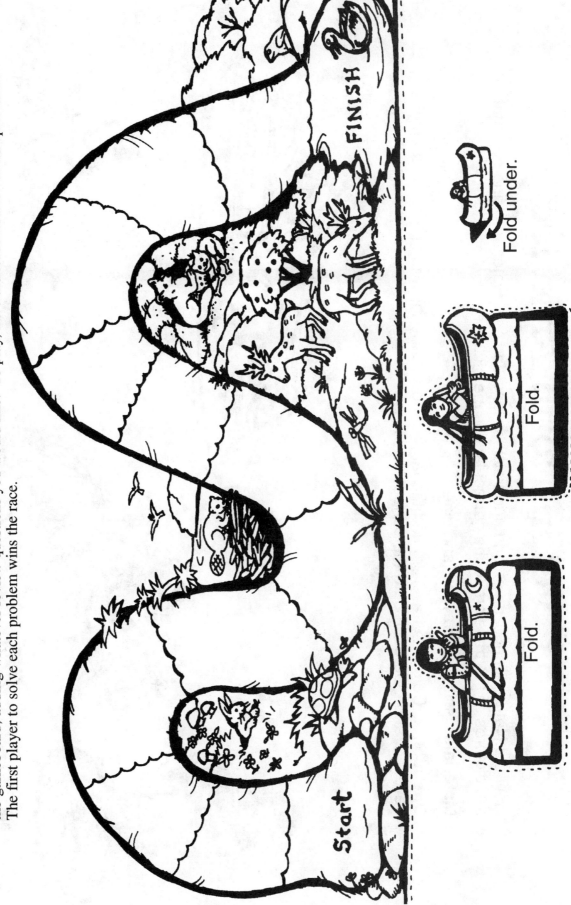

Fold under.

Fold.

Fold.

FINISH

Start

Travel in North America

How did Native Americans of long ago travel by land and over water? To find out, match the pictures of the travelers to the correct landscape pictures.

Materials: scissors, crayons, and glue

Directions: Color the travellers and the landscapes on the following page. Cut out the travellers and glue each onto the correct landscape.

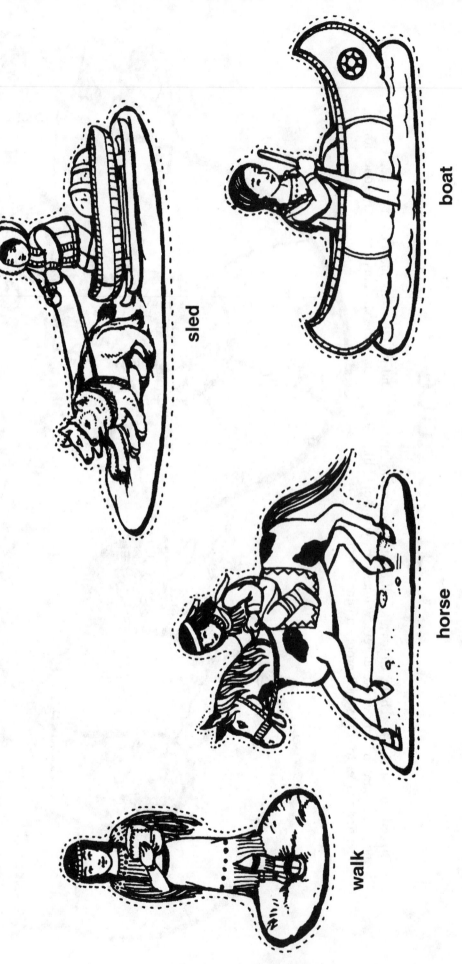

sled

boat

horse

walk

Name _____

Travel in North America *(cont.)*

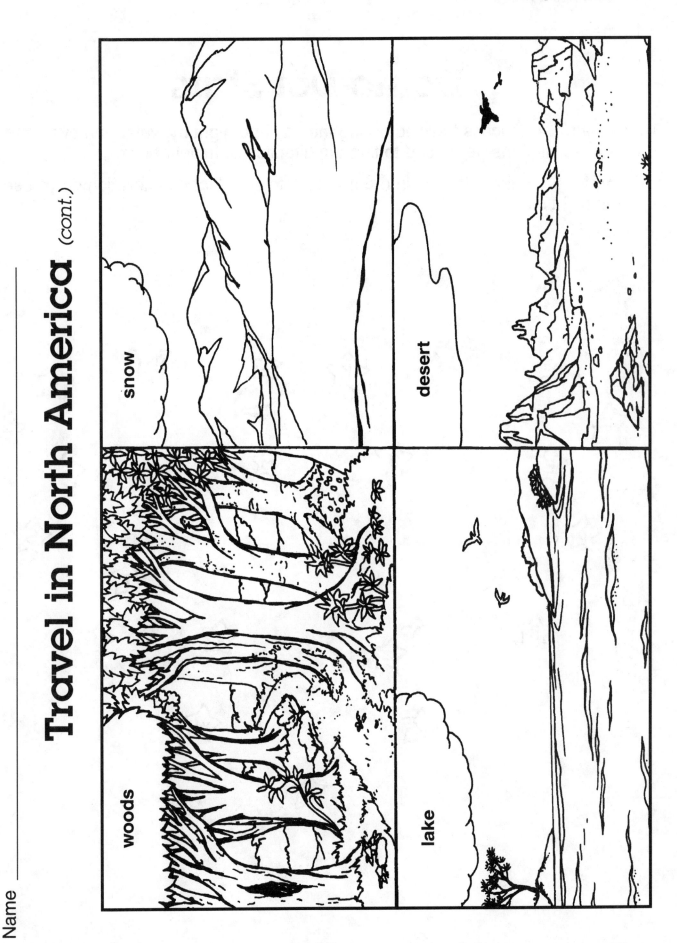

snow

desert

woods

lake

Name _____

Dot-to-Dot Stars

The Native Americans traveled during the day and night by water and over land. Star constellations were used to find the direction of travel at night.

Directions: Follow the dots in order from A to Z. What constellation do you see in the night sky?

Name _____

Measure the Boats

Directions: Use the canoe ruler to measure the length of each boat. Write the answer in the square next to each boat.

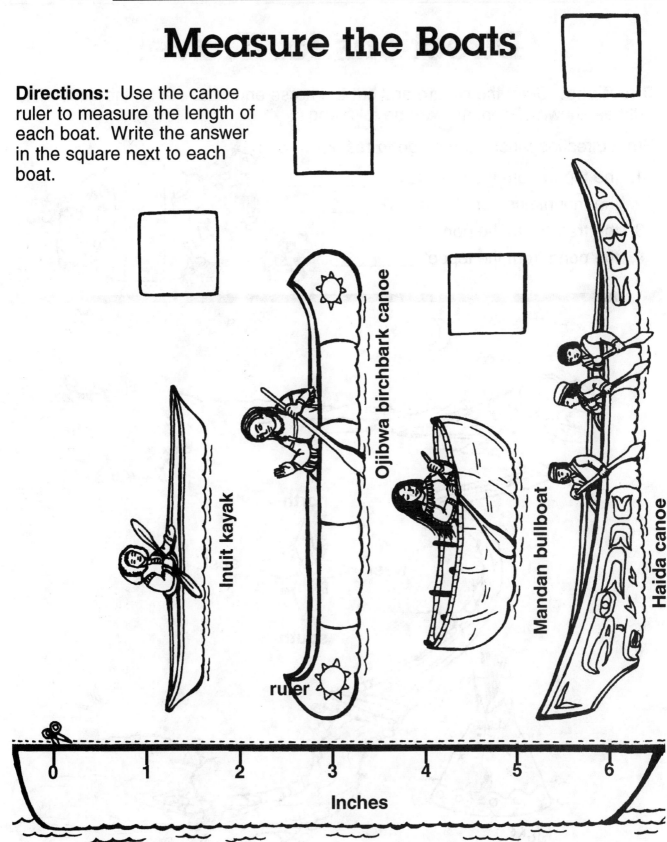

Inuit kayak

Ojibwa birchbark canoe

ruler

Mandan bullboat

Haida canoe

Inches

Name _____

Directions for Travel

Directions: Color the picture and cut the horse and rider out on the dotted line. Fold as shown. Then, answer the following.

What direction must the rider go to reach . . .

1. the tepee from the mountains? _____
2. the mountains from the trees? _____
3. the trees from the pond? _____
4. the pond from the tepee? _____

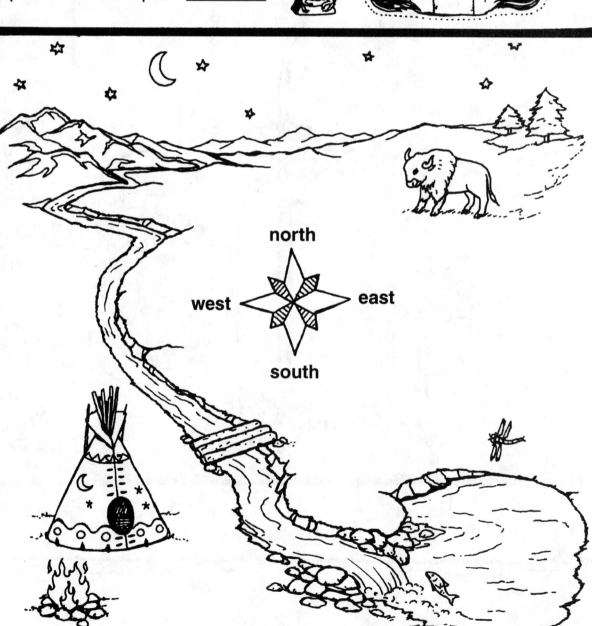

Communication

The Universal Necessity of Communication

Communication is a basic need for all people. It may be achieved through such methods as speech, the printed word, song, dance, drama, sign language, and symbols. Thoughts, ideas, and feelings are exchanged both verbally and nonverbally, and thoughts and feelings will arise spontaneously in a person as a reaction to words, sounds, sights, smells, touches, or memories.

When one person is motivated to express thoughts to another, communication can occur. It is also possible to communicate feelings and thoughts unintentionally, through body language or tone of voice, and a single word can have many meanings, depending upon the situation and each individual's frame of mind.

Communication skills such as reading, speaking, and writing are the major focus of educational curriculum at all levels, as well they should be since communication is the vehicle that allows individuals to relate to one another. The functionality of a society often depends upon its ability to communicate.

A Land of Many Languages

By the 17th century, over six hundred Native American dialects were spoken across the North American continent. The major language groups were Hokan, Macro-Algonquin, Macro-Sioran, NaDene, Pennutian, Macro-Chibchan, and Macro-Otomanguean. The People within each language group were generally able to understand one another when they spoke. Because of the existence of so many dialects, it was necessary to establish universal methods of communication that did not rely upon speech. People from different areas needed to communicate with one another when they met for trade, hunted game across mutually shared grazing lands, or celebrated special occasions such as dance and ritual ceremonies. Words were viewed as powerful tools which could be used to bring the rain, to ensure a successful hunt, or to please the Great Spirit.

Communication (cont.)

Communication Among Animals

Animals communicate through sounds and body language. Most animals live in groups where the survival of the many depends upon communication and cooperation among individuals. Whales beneath the ocean exchange distinct messages by producing high-pitched calls which protect the younger whales from harm. Birds in the air cry out as they fly, alerting other birds of their approach. Bees give direction to a field of flowers by walking in predictable formation inside the hive. The other bees then fly to the indicated flower patch. Dogs and cats have a broad range of sounds and gestures which reveal their pleasure or displeasure. Some monkeys have adopted sign language taught them by humans. Among all of the animals on earth, only humans have such a refined and vast range of communication skills. Only humans create artworks and poetry. The human brain has evolved to store, encode, and retrieve information on a level which rivals any computer. All healthy infants are capable of learning any language and of responding to such universal modes of communication as a smiling face and soothing music.

The Necessity of Communication Among Early Native Americans

On many occasions, early Native Americans found it necessary to establish communication among various groups. Travel, trade, territorial treaties, and special ceremonies such as weddings and seasonal celebrations brought together people from various language groups. When verbal communication was not possible, other methods of communication were used. The most common was sign language.

Communication with Plants and Animals

All plants and animals living on earth today share a common ancestry in the distant past. Animals and plants are traditionally viewed as important helpers for humans. Without plants and animals to eat, humans could not survive. Therefore, whenever early Native Americans gathered plants, they said a prayer or offered a gift in exchange for the help of the plant. When an animal was hunted, prayers and a small gift were offered to the animal for allowing the humans to eat its flesh and use its fur, hide, and bones. Native Americans never took something from nature without expressing gratitude and respect for it.

Communication (cont.)

Methods of Communication

Calendars, Time Keeping, and Navigation

Time passage was recorded on calendar sticks, wall murals, astronomical stone circles, caves, and paintings. Agricultural calendars were divided by the summer and winter solstice to indicate planting and harvesting schedules. Astronomical observations of constellations, moon cycles, and the position of the sun guided navigation during the day or night travel. Pictographs of planets and star constellations were etched or painted onto cave walls, kiva murals, tepees, shields, and clothing. The protection of the sun, moon, and stars was requested through prayers and the offering of gifts.

Trail Markers

Travelers often followed "signs" such as trail markers in the woods which indicated passageways, water, animal habitats, and territorial designations. When nomadic hunters set out to follow a herd of grazing animals, they sometimes buried the possessions not needed for their journey. A special identification stick was then left at the site so that others would know that the possessions had not been abandoned by their owner.

Drum Signals

Drums made from hollowed tree trunks, clay pots, and stretched animal skins were used to send messages among groups and individuals, even at great distances. The strength and frequency of the drum beats conveyed a commonly recognized code.

Smoke Signals

Smoking fires were used to send smoke signals across the sky. Moist branches were burned in order to ensure thick smoke which was then released in long and short puffs. A blanket was waved across the smoke fire to control the message.

Wampum Belts

Wampum belts were usually made from clamshell beads of purple and white color. Some belts were five feet (1.5 m) long or more. The patterns formed by the colored beads recorded and commemorated certain events such as treaties, weddings, or successful hunts. Wampum belts were a popular trade item.

Birchbark Scrolls

Birchbark scrolls were used by the People of the Woodlands. The birchbark was peeled from the trees and then etched or painted with symbols and pictures.

Symbolic Icons and Pictographs

Symbolic icons and pictographs were etched and painted onto tepees, sculptures, shields, blankets, rugs, baskets and pottery. These images depicted human and animal names, objects, events, and ideas.

Communication *(cont.)*

Methods of Communication *(cont.)*

Sacred Names

Children were given names at birth as well as during special stages of their lives, for example, when they reached puberty or completed their first successful hunt. Special names were also given when a vision or a dream with a message from the spirit realm was received. These secret names often alluded to the animal which appeared in the dream. Many clan names also used animal names and images. Animals were often called honorable names. For example, the bear was called "Old Grandfather" or "The One Who Possesses Healing Wisdom." This was done to honor and to please the bear. Names and images were considered to be powerful tools for gaining physical strength as well as spiritual blessings.

Color Symbolism

Colors played an important role in communication. Symbolic meaning was given to colors appearing in nature, dreams, prayers, poems, and origin myths. Colors have the power to delight, transform, provoke, or soothe. Animals, people, plants, directions, deities, and spirit messengers were all associated with specific colors.

Oral Narration

Origin stories which described the original creation of the world, animals, plants, and humans were conveyed by oral narration. Most early Native Americans did not possess a formal written language. Traditional knowledge and skills were therefore preserved in the memory of special storytellers who were cued by recorded symbols, colors, and pictures as they spoke. Poems and stories were often sung and danced in special ceremonies. The greatest narrators were considered very important within each society because of their ability to entertain and educate.

Healing Ceremonies

When a child or an adult became ill, healing ceremonies were arranged to make that person well. These ceremonies were performed in order to communicate with the spirits or forces of nature associated with the medicinal arts, such as the Bear Spirit.

The Navajo of the Southwest continue their ancient practice of sandpainting ceremonies. During this ceremony, the person who needs treatment sits upon a sandpainting prepared with crushed stone, shells, and plants. The sandpainting is prepared at dawn and then destroyed at sundown after the prayers, herbal medicines, and incense offerings have been completed.

Extension Activities

1. Students can "decode" pictures made from a word list.
2. Students may write messages using traditional and original picture writing and sign language.
3. Students can compare modern picture symbols such as traffic signs and international airport signs with traditional picture writing.

Topics for Discussion

Discuss the need for communication as well as the methods of communication employed in the past and the present. Use some or all of the following questions for discussion topics.

1. What does it mean to communicate?
2. What methods do we use today to communicate with each other?
3. Why is communication important to us?
4. How does communication among humans and among animals differ?
5. How is communication among humans and among animals alike?
6. When and how do we use words today?
7. How would we communicate without spoken words?
8. How did the early Native Americans communicate with one another?
   (sign language, spoken words, songs, poetry, pictographs, painting, etc.)
9. What technologies do we use these days for communication?
10. What is an origin myth or explanation?
11. How did the early Native Americans communicate with each other when they met someone who spoke a different language?
    (sign language, dance, offering of gifts, etc.)
12. How did the early Native Americans communicate over long distance?
    (smoke signals, drum signals, trail markings, etc.)
13. What is a pictograph?
    (a picture which gives information, like a symbol)
14. What uses do we have for picture symbols today?
15. What uses did the early Native Americans have for symbols?
    (trail markings, treaties, trade, dream/vision art, decoration of tepees, shields, clothing, jewelry, etc.)
16. Have you ever made up a secret code or personal symbol for your own use?

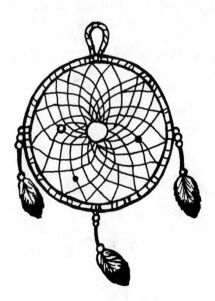

Activities for Communication

The following activities can be used with pages 125-136.

Poetry

The students can write poems and inscribe them on one of the patterns provided.

Oral Narration

Each student can tell one segment of a story, allowing other students to take turns adding their own twists to the ongoing narration.

Origin Myths

Students can listen to traditional stories of creation and the origin of specific animals, land or water masses, groups of people, and so forth. The students may then write and illustrate their own stories which explain the beginning of some natural component of our world.

While doing this activity, please be sure to discuss with students the fact that virtually every culture has its own explanation for the origins of the world and the people and things within it. For many, such explanations are a firm part of the cultural history, and a suggestion that such explanations may be stories and not concrete fact can prove highly offensive.

Sign Language

Students can study traditional sign language and then compare it to modern sign language used by hearing impaired persons. Students can also create their own sign language.

Symbols and Pictographs

Students can review symbols and pictographs which were used by early Native Americans. These can then be used to write a message which other students can decipher.

Examples of modern symbols may be reviewed and discussed. For example, hundreds of icons have been created to inform people where to eat, park, or sit, or when to walk, stop, go, and so forth.

Students may also create a new system of symbols in order to send messages to one another.

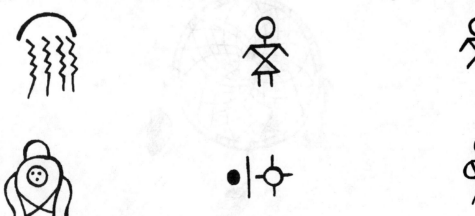

Birchbark Scroll

In the Woodlands, birchbark scrolls were used to send messages.

Directions: Write your own message on the birchbark scroll below. Roll it up and tie it with a piece of yarn. Deliver it to a friend.

Sandpainting

Sandpaintings were made in the Southwest pueblos. Navaho medicine healers made designs with colored sand. Stones, corn pollen, and shells were also used in powdered form. To make your own sandpainting, follow these directions.

Materials: colored sand (purchase from a store or color with vegetable dyes), white glue, 8" (20 cm) cardboard square, crayons, and the sample design (page 127)

Directions: Draw an original design on your cardboard square or use the design on the next page. Color the design with crayons. Cover one colored area with glue and sprinkle colored sand on the glue. When the glue is dry, shake off the extra sand. Then, repeat the glue-and-sand steps for each color. When your sandpainting is complete, give it a title.

Sample Sandpainting Design

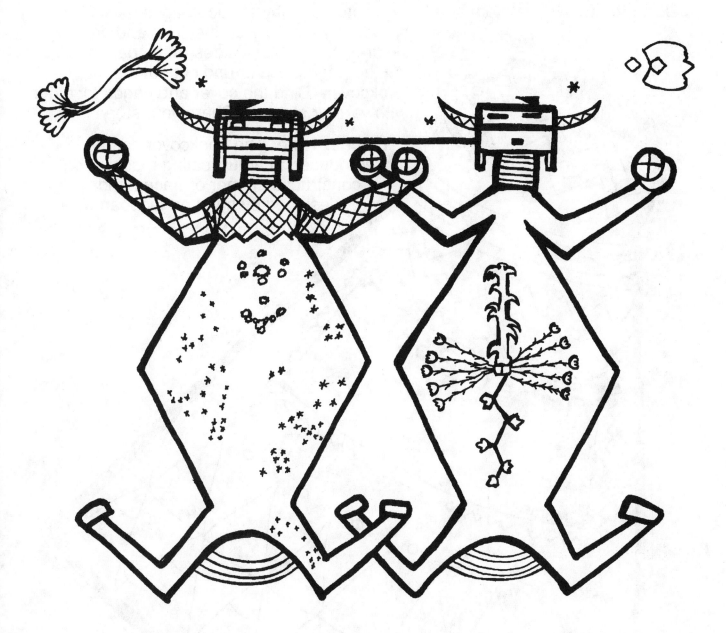

Father Sky, Mother Earth

Tepee-Shaped Book

Materials: patterns (pages 128-129), tagboard or construction paper*, paper, scissors, crayons, a pencil, and a stapler or yarn and a hole punch

Directions: Write a story and copy it onto as many shaped pages as necessary. Write your story on the lines and draw pictures on the blank sides of the pages. Cut out the pages. Color and cut out the bookcover. Bind the cover and pages together with yarn or staples. Share your story!

*Teacher Note: The bookcover can be reproduced in a duplicating machine on construction paper or traced and designed by hand on tagboard.

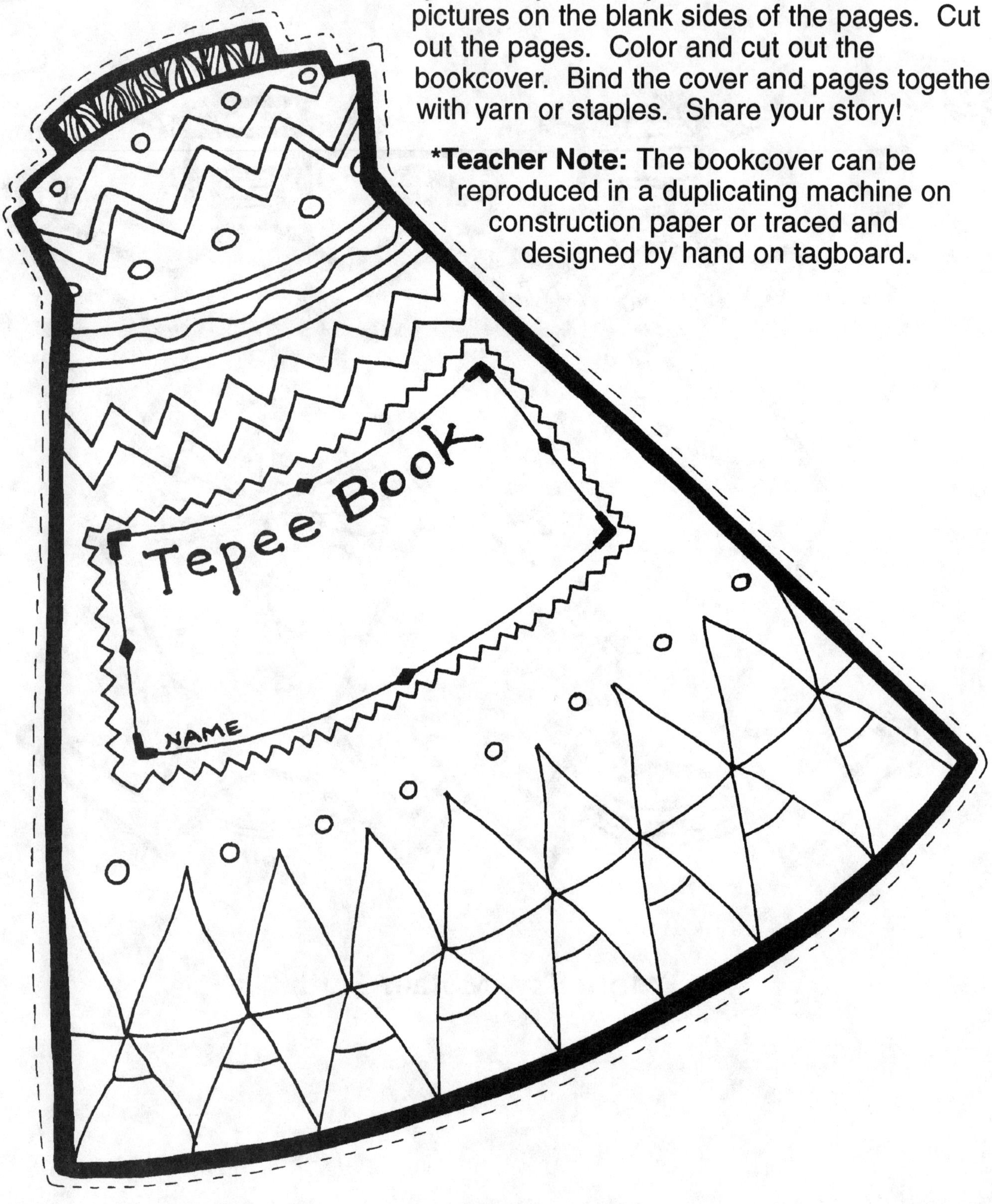

Tepee Book

NAME

Tepee-Shaped Book (cont.)

Name _____

Smoke Signals

Smoke signals were sent over long distances by waving a wet blanket over a smoking fire so that short or long puffs of smoke would be sent into the air. The idea is similar to Morse code or semaphore, where signals are used to communicate.

Directions: Write and draw your own smoke signal below.

Picture Writing of the Great Plains

Over thirty dialects were spoken across the Great Plains area. Universal picture symbols were used to record events, tell stories, send messages, and as designs on tepees and clothing. Following are some examples. Use them for your own designs or in your own communications.

Sign Language

Hundreds of dialects were spoken across North America. Universal sign language was often used to communicate among people who did not speak the same language. Following are some examples. Practice them until you know them by heart.

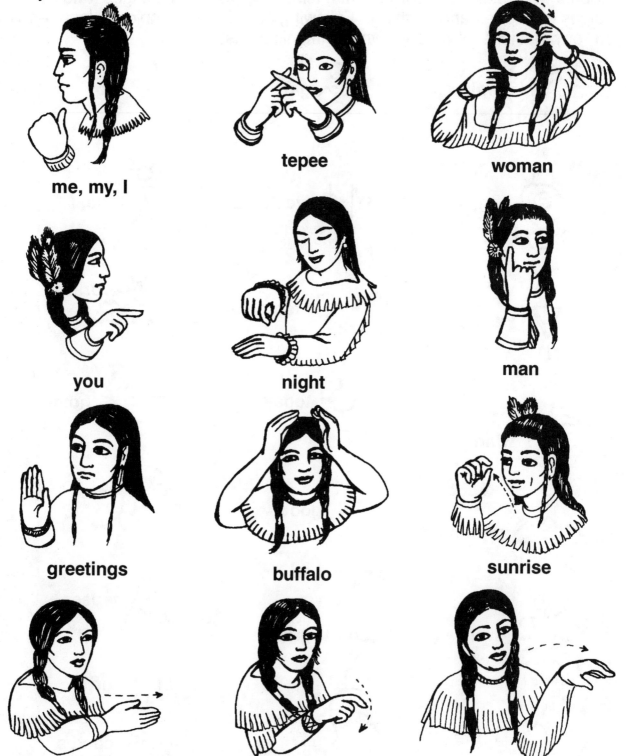

me, my, I

tepee

woman

you

night

man

greetings

buffalo

sunrise

go away

yes

sunset

Name _____

Writing Border

Directions: Write a poem and print it inside the border. Draw a picture to illustrate your poem.

Dream Catcher

Dream catchers are woven hoops placed over a child's bed or cradleboard as the child sleeps. They are said to have originated with the Oneida in the northeastern United States. The hoops are decorated with shells, feathers, beads, and ribbons. Bad dreams are "captured" by the dream catcher, but good dreams pass through to the sleeper.

Follow these directions to make your own dream catcher.

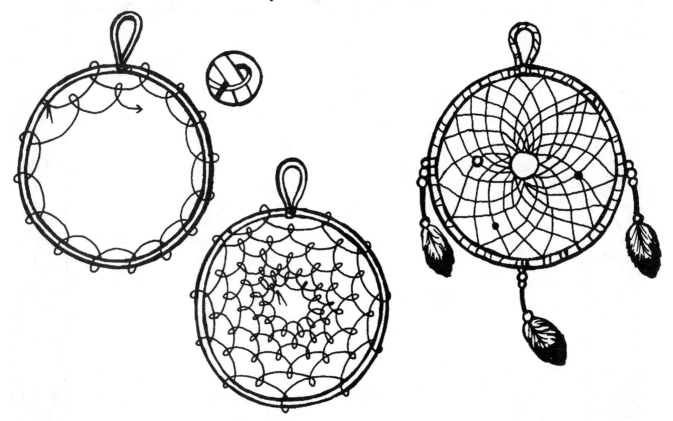

Materials: wire clothes hanger; string, yarn, ribbon, or leather thonging; beads, shells, feathers, or other items for decoration

Directions: Bend the hanger into a hoop. Wrap string (or another material) around the hoop.

Tie one end of string to the hoop. Proceed around the hoop at even intervals, wrapping the string as shown. Keep the string pulled snug. When you have gone around the entire circle, start the next set of wraps in the center of the first wrap made. (See illustration.)

Continue around until only a small circle remains open in the center of the hoop. Tie off the string. Decorate the dream catcher as desired with beads, shells, etc.

My Dream

Directions: Write your dream in the dream catcher and draw a picture to illustrate it. Color and cut it out.

Bookmarks

Directions: Design a bookmark of your own and then color and cut out all three.

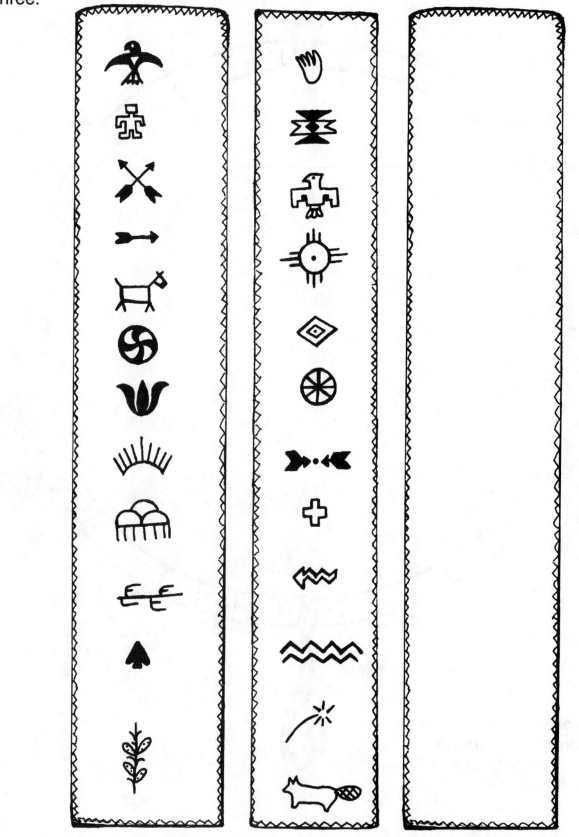

Clothing and Jewelry

Clothing for Protection

Clothing and jewelry are worn by people of all cultures. Clothing is worn as protection from rain, snow, and desert heat. Clothing is often decorated with colors, patterns, or textures, either printed or woven. Those who live in cold climates wear furs or woolen garments. People living in warm climates generally wear cotton or other plant fiber garments. Cotton and wool have been woven for thousands of years and continue to be the major clothing fiber in most countries. Polyester, rayon, and nylon fibers are also woven into fabric in our present day.

Clothing and Jewelry as Adornment and Symbol

Since prehistoric times, stones, shells, feathers, and metals have been used as decoration and worn on the wrist, neck, finger, ankle, ear, or waistline. Bones, antlers, teeth, claws, and fur have provided materials for jewelry as well.

Both clothing and jewelry have been used in the past to communicate information about the wearer or to honor certain events and holidays. For example, a queen or empress in Europe or Asia traditionally wore fine silk garments and precious colored gems to show her identity. In ancient Greece, only the wealthy class was allowed to wear the color purple. In the mountains of Tibet, red robes and turquoise rosaries were worn by the Buddhist monks and nuns. The Chinese Imperial families reserved the right to wear canary yellow silk robes embroidered with flying dragons. In Korea, Buddhist monks and nuns wear gray robes. The priests and nuns of the Catholic Church often wear black clothing and crosses to identify themselves.

In most countries today, special clothing is worn for weddings, holidays, and funerals. Police officers, firefighters, and medical professionals wear special uniforms and badges for identification. Some schools and sports teams have their own uniforms and rings. Ribbons and medals are worn by military personnel to symbolize rank and heroic deeds. A white bridal dress and a gold wedding band are customary in modern America. In India, a bride wears a red sari and a gold necklace.

Traditional Clothes Today

Modern children often have certain clothing set aside for special events and special occasions. Sometimes this clothing is part of their cultural heritage. Many contemporary Native American children have such special clothing. However, on a regular basis, Native American children today dress just as children from other cultures do.

As a way to celebrate, honor, and keep alive their heritage, many contemporary Native American artisans make jewelry and textiles by using traditional materials or designs in new or traditional ways.

Clothing and Jewelry *(cont.)*

The Traditional Clothing of the Native Americans

The climate and available materials determined the type of clothing worn by early Native Americans. If the climate was cold and snowy, the skins and furs of animals were used to make gloves, coats, hats, pants, shirts, skirts, boots, and bedding. The people of the Far North and Arctic regions wore softened animal hides and furs all year long. In the coldest winter months, two layers of fur clothing were worn. The inner layer of clothing was worn with the fur against the body while the outer layer was worn with the fur facing out.

Where the climate was hot, as in the Southwest and Southeast, clothes were made from woven cotton, bark, yucca, moss, and other plant fibers. Sandals were woven from yucca fibers, as well. Moccasins were worn when traveling. In summer, the women, men, and children often walked barefoot.

The clothing in cold climates was generally tailored to fit the body snugly. This allowed easier movement with less weight. In the warmer climates the clothing tended to be loose for greater coolness and comfort.

Across North America, painting and tattooing of the face and body with patterns and colors was common.

Women: Textile Artisans

It was usually the women who sewed and decorated the clothing worn by the men, children, and themselves. Needles were often made from animal bones or ivory. Sinew or plant fibers were used as thread. Most women possessed a sewing kit, which itself was a work of art. Great artistic skill and patience were required to prepare the plant fibers or animal skins, sew or weave them, and then decorate the garments with paint, quill work, beads, shells, and ribbon applique. The entire dress, shirt, papoose cradle, bag, or moccasin was sometimes covered with an embroidery of porcupine quills and beads. The women of the Great Plains and the Eastern Woodlands were famous for their beautiful paintings, bead, and quill embroidery. Geometric as well as floral designs were popular. The girls and women took great pride in their textile arts skills.

Boys and men sometimes painted tepees and special garments, such as the medicine shirts or buffalo robes. Some Hopi men also wove cotton and wool on looms. However, the majority of clothing, rugs, sashes, robes, blankets, and household items was prepared and decorated by women.

Clothing and Jewelry *(cont.)*

Seasonal Clothing Across North America

In the Midwestern regions, clothing changed with the season. Long fringe was cut into the leggings, shirts, and dresses made from buckskin. Heavy furs and blankets were worn in the winter while the summer months required only lightweight animal skins as clothing material. The people of the subtropical Southeastern regions wore woven grass capes and skirts. The people of the Northwest Pacific Coast wore wool from caribou or mountain goats blended with bark fibers and woven on looms for robes, capes, and blankets.

Materials used for clothing included animal skins and furs, grass fibers such as hemp, and wool from goats, dogs, moose, caribou and sheep. (Sheep were domesticated animals brought from Europe. The Native Americans readily adapted to using their wool.) The soft inner bark of trees was used as clothing fiber in the Great Basin region as well as along the Northwest Pacific Coast. Some capes in the Southwest and Southeast were woven with colored feathers as in the Incan tradition.

Materials Used for Jewelry

Jewelry was made from local materials such as seeds, shells, and animals bones, as well as from materials traded over long distances. For example, shells such as clam, abalone, and cowrie were brought from the California and Southeast Coasts to the interior, and porcupine quills were brought down from the northern regions to be traded on the Plains and the Woodlands where they were used for jewelry and clothing decoration. Feathers, animal teeth and hair, claws, antlers, bones, ivory, shells, stones, and fur pieces were used for jewelry and for decoration on clothing, tepees, shields, blankets, and carrying vessels. Turquoise, ivory, jet, mother of pearl, and jade were all used for beads. The beads were drilled with holes and then strung on thin sinew or string. Silverwork set with coral, turquoise, and other stones were made by the pueblo people of the Southwest. Necklaces, bracelets, rings, pendants, earrings, belts, and brooches were made by the Hopi, Zuni, and Navaho artisans who continue this tradition today.

Clothing and Jewelry (cont.)

The Preparation of Animal Skins

Across North America, animal skins were prepared in a similar manner. The skins were generally cleaned, prepared, and decorated by the women. The animals were skinned and the hide was scraped with a tool until the skin was of uniform thickness. The fur was either left on the skin or scraped off. The cleaned hide was then stretched onto a frame or pegged to the ground with wooden stakes. The hide was allowed to dry out and rubbed with special oil mixtures to soften the leather. The tanning process could take over a week of hard work until the hide was ready for sewing and decorating. The finished hide was then removed from the stretchers and cut and sewn into clothing. The finished garments were decorated with paint, embroidery, or applique designs. The hides were used for clothing, tepee coverings, carrying bags, shields, and cooking vessels.

Some animal hides were heated by fire until they became very tough. Arrows and even bullets could not penetrate the leather shields which were prepared in this manner.

Textile Weaving

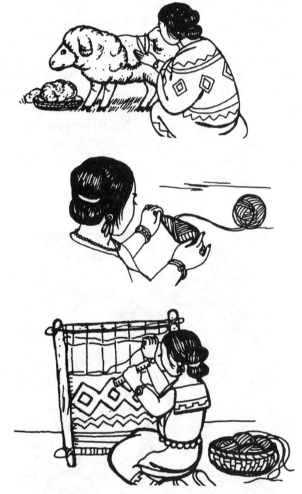

The steps of weaving are the same everywhere. Plant or wool fibers are gathered for weaving, or when wool is used, the animal is sheared of its woolen coat. The wool is then cleaned and prepared for the loom by twisting it onto a spindle as yarn. The yarn may then be dyed with vegetable or mineral dyes, and in recent times, with aniline dyes. The yarn is then woven on a loom with a warp made from string or wool. The yarn is then drawn through the warp strings, forming the weft. Designs are made with colors, textures, and patterns. Complex weaving patterns can produce a different pattern on each side of the fabric.

Many items were woven by the early Native Americans. These included rugs, blankets, sashes, dresses, carrying bags, and hats. From shearing the sheep to creating the finished product, over four hundred hours of work were required to produce a three by five feet (1 x 1.5 m) rug.

Woven blankets and rugs were traded to Europeans during the eighteenth century. Geometric and floral designs were sometimes made from old Asian and European motifs in order to accommodate the tastes of the European traders.

Natural Textile Dyes

Roots, bark, minerals, and plants were used to create natural textile dyes to color wool, porcupine quills, and plant fibers. Designs were also made from naturally colored wool, which ranges from black, white, gray, and cream to shades of brown. The earliest pueblo blankets were designed with stripes of various widths and colors. The students may enjoy preparing some textile dyes in the traditional manner using local materials such as berries and bark.

Topics for Discussion

Discuss the design and purpose of clothing, textile arts, and jewelry of the past and present. Use some or all of the following questions for discussion topics.

1. Are clothes necessary? Why do people wear clothing?
2. Why do people wear jewelry and other adornments (such as badges or medals)?
3. What kinds of clothes do we wear?
4. When do we wear special clothing?
5. Who makes our clothes?
6. What are our clothes and jewelry made from?
7. Do our clothes have different colors and designs? Why?
8. Do we change our wardrobes at different times of the year? When?
9. What kinds of clothing do people in other countries wear?
10. What kinds of clothing did the early Native Americans wear?
    (moccasins, headdresses, hats, leggings, vests, dresses, shirts, etc.)
11. What kinds of textile arts did the early Native Americans make?
    (woven blankets, rugs, dresses, carrying bags, etc.)
12. What materials were used for their textile arts?
    (cotton, wool from various animals, plant fibers, furs, etc.)
13. What materials were used for traditional clothing and jewelry by the Native Americans?
    (fur, animal hides, cotton, plant fibers, and wool for clothing; antlers, ivory, bones, claws, feathers, shells, beads, and metals for jewelry)
14. Did any of the traditional Native American clothing and jewelry have any special or symbolic meaning?
    (Have the students do some research to answer this question. They will find, for example, that the feathers which were used in headdresses were symbolic of special events.)

Southwestern Jewelry

The Hopi, Zuni, and Navaho made silver jewelry for everyday wear and for special occasions. Southwestern jewelry was an important trade item in the past and continues to be made by modern artisans. Silver jewelry is set with stones and shells.

To make your own paper jewelry, follow these directions.

Materials: crayons, scissors, tape, and string

Directions: Color the stones on your paper jewelry with coral red, turquoise blue, and jet black. Cut on the dotted lines and tape or string as shown.

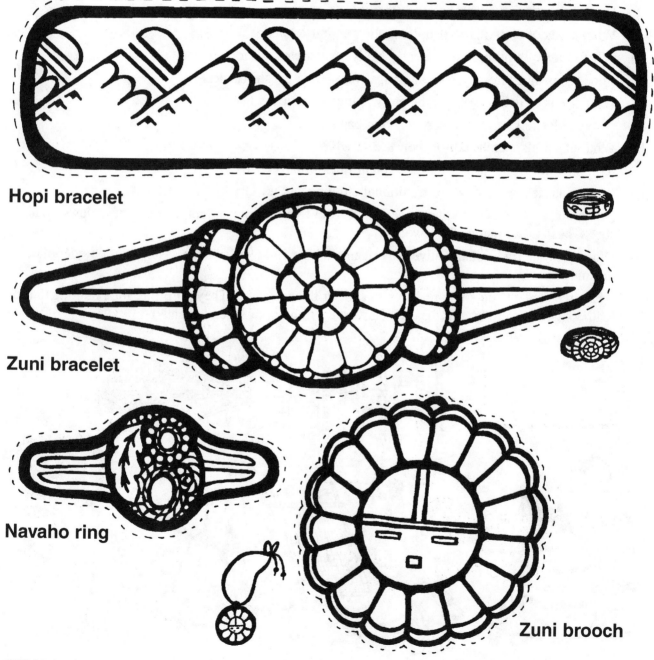

Hopi bracelet

Zuni bracelet

Navaho ring

Zuni brooch

Weave on a Loom

In the Southwest pueblos, rugs and blankets were woven on looms. Wool from dogs, goats, and sheep was spun into yarn on a spindle and then woven on a wooden loom.

Make your own weaving on a cardboard loom. Follow the directions below.

Materials: 8" x 12" (20 cm x 30 cm) cardboard rectangle, scissors, yarn, and tape

Directions:

1. Cut small notches along the top and bottom edges of the cardboard loom.

2. Wrap yarn through each notch as shown. This is the warp. Tie or tape the yarn ends.

3. Weave the colored yarn back and forth through the warp. This is the weft. Weave a design with colored yarns.

4. Cut and tie the warp ends. Then remove your weaving from the loom.

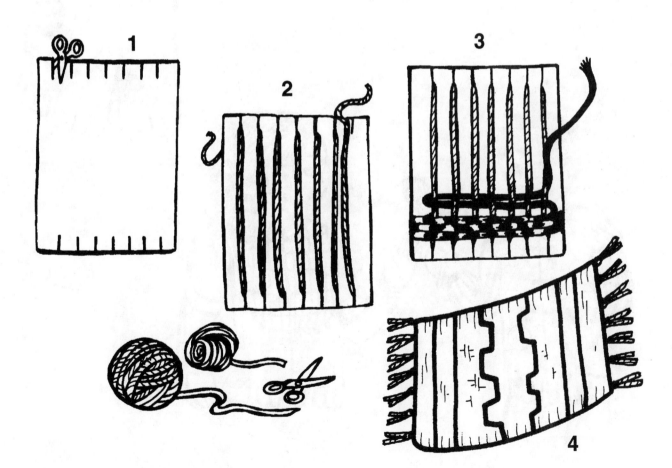

Paper Bag Vest

Vests made from animal skins were worn in the Great Plains and in the Eastern Woodlands. Some vests were decorated with porcupine quills or beads. Fringe was cut along the edge of the hem. The fringe was a symbol of the rays of light which come from each person's spirit.

Make your own vest from a paper bag.

Materials: large brown paper grocery bag, scissors, crayons or paint, and beads, yarn, feathers, ribbons, shells, or colored macaroni

Directions: Open the bag. Draw a neck circle on the bottom, an arm circle on each side, and a line up the center of your paper bag for the vest opening. Cut the center line from the bottom of the bag to the neck circle. Cut out the neck and arm circles.

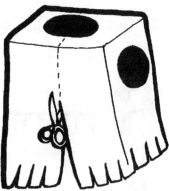

To decorate your vest, color pictures and designs and cut fringe on the bottom. Add beads, yarn, feathers, ribbons, shells, and/or macaroni for adornment.

A Navaho Weaver

Materials: crayons, scissors, yarn, and tape

Directions: Color and cut out the picture of the weaving Navaho woman. Tape a piece of yarn to her basket. Cut out the arm and attach it to her shoulder with a paper fastener (brad). Tape the piece of yarn to the woman's moving hand and watch her weave!

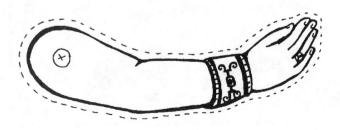

Name _____

Match the Moccasins

Early Native Americans wore leather moccasins decorated with porcupine quills and beads. Some moccasins were for the winter, and others were worn in the summer.

Directions: Match the moccasins in every square with the one in each row that looks the same. Color each pair.

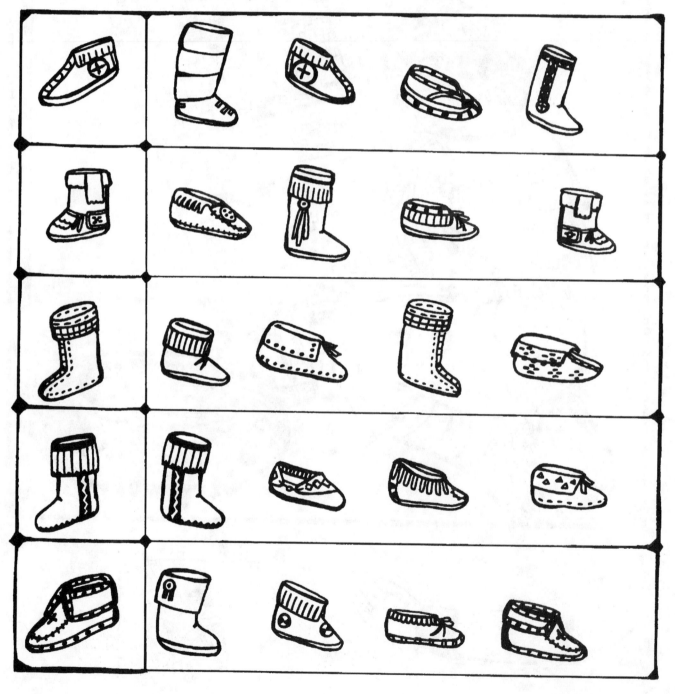

Name _____

Painted Buffalo Robe

Buffalo hide robes were worn across the Great Plains, Southwest, and Eastern Woodlands. These robes were painted with geometric designs and pictures from the life of the wearer (both men and women).

Directions: Decorate this buffalo skin robe with colors and pictures that have some special meaning to you.

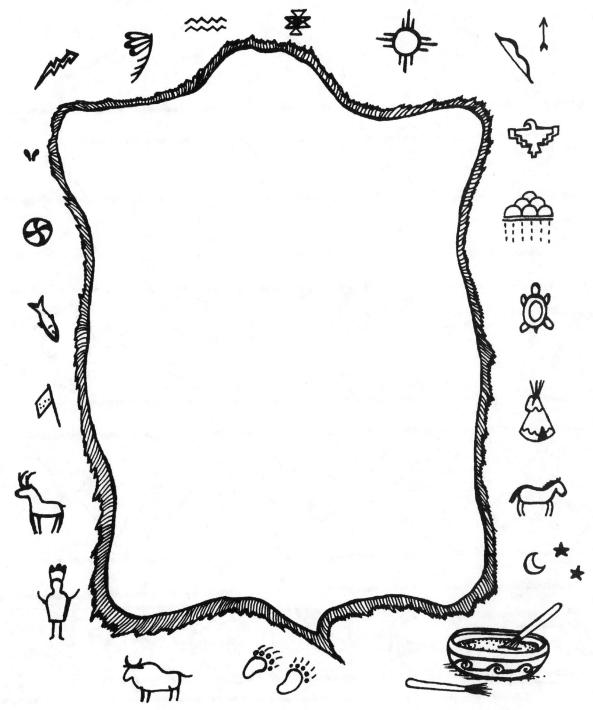

Border Designs

Porcupines quills, beads, and paint were used to make borders on clothing in the Great Plains and Eastern Woodlands. Some designs took many days to complete.

Directions: Color the border designs below and design one of your own. Cut the borders out. Paste them on bookcovers or use them as bookmarks.

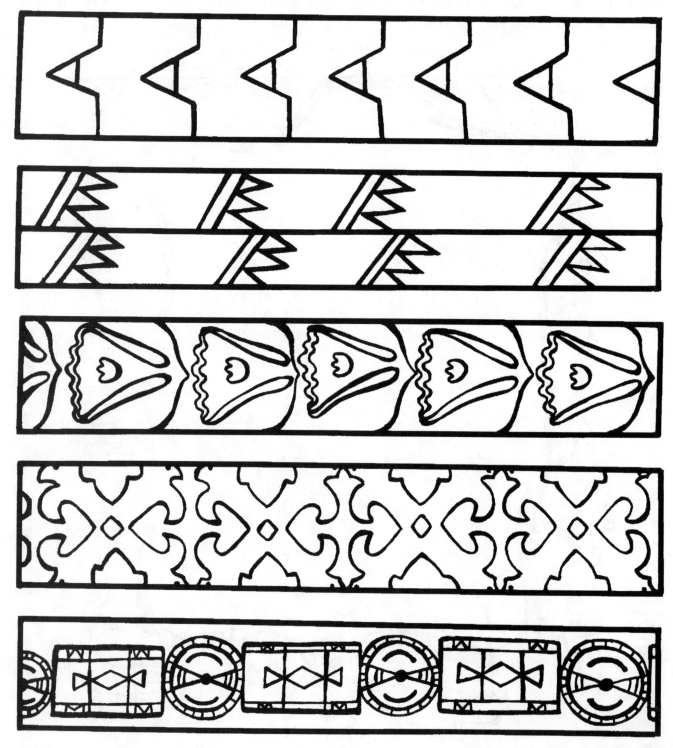

Weaving a Rug

Directions: Color and cut the squares below. Paste them in correct order on a long paper strip.

Wash the wool.

Display the rug.

Weave on the loom.

Cut the wool.

Remove the rug from the loom.

Spin the wool on a spindle.

Clothing Styles of the Southwest Pueblos

Directions: Color and cut out the figures and clothing.

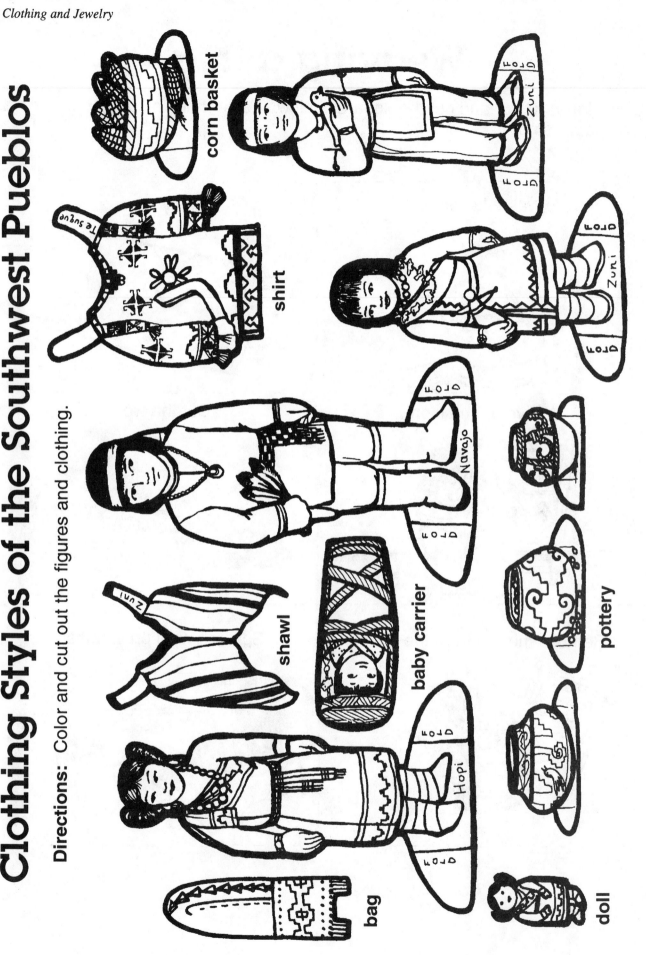

corn basket

shirt

Zuni

Zuni

Te sugue

Navajo

shawl

Zuni

baby carrier

pottery

Hopi

bag

doll

Clothing Styles of the Pacific Northwest and California

Directions: Color and cut out the figures and clothing.

shawl

bowl

comb

hats

box

baskets

Clothing Styles of the Arctic and Far North

Directions: Color and cut out the figures and clothing.

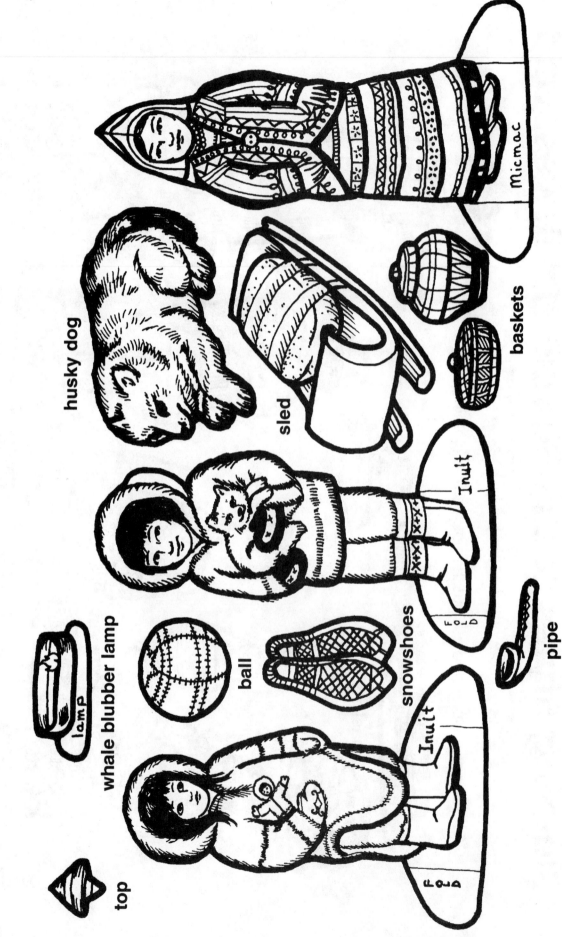

husky dog

sled

baskets

Micmac

Inuit

snowshoes

pipe

ball

whale blubber lamp

lamp

top

Inuit

Clothing Styles of the Great Plains

Directions: Color and cut out the figures and clothing.

Sioux

baskets

bag

parfleche

doll

necklace

spoon

Sioux

Dakota

shield

sewing bag

Clothing Styles of the Woodlands

Directions: Color and cut out the figures and clothing.

baskets

wampum

Iroquois

FOLD

FOLD

tomahawk

Sauk chief

box

comb

carrying bag

baby carrier

pipe

seminole

FOLD

Seminole

FOLD

bowls

FOLD

The Gift of the Spiderwoman

A Hopi Legend of the Origin of the Weaving Arts
retold by Mary E. Connors

In a time long ago, the People did not weave cloth.
They did not know of the loom and spindle.

No one knew, only She.
It was She who spun the web which ties the clouds to the sky.

It was She who spins on a loom of rainbows.
It was She who lives in a house with four doors and four ladders.

On the East stands a ladder of white shell.
On the West stands a ladder of turquoise.

On the South stands a ladder of red shell.
On the North stands a ladder of black jet.

In the center She sits spinning on her loom of rainbows.
Her home is filled with weavings of all colors and patterns.

She has spun them all on her spindle.
She has woven them all on her loom.

Her husband, the Sun, is pleased when he sees them.
It was She, Spiderwoman.

Spiderwoman taught White-Shell-Woman the secrets of weaving.
White-Shell-Woman watched Spiderwoman weaving on her rainbow loom.

For four days White-Shell-Woman watched.
White-Shell-Woman returned to her Earth Surface People.

There, she made a loom of wood and yarn.
There, she shared the secrets she had learned.

In this way the Earth Surface People received the gift of Kokyangwuti,
the Spiderwoman.

(Teacher Note: This is an enlarged and unified version of the story told in the minibook on
pages 156–162.)

The Gift of the Spiderwoman

A Hopi Legend of the Origin of the Weaving Arts
retold by Mary E. Connors

In a time long ago, the People did not weave cloth.
They did not know of the loom and spindle.

No one knew, only She.
It was She who spun the web which ties the clouds to the sky.

It was She who spins on a loom of rainbows.
It was She who lives in a house with four doors and four ladders.

On the East stands a ladder of white shell.
On the West stands a ladder of turquoise.

4

On the South stands a ladder of red shell.
On the North stands a ladder of black jet.

5

In the center She sits spinning on her loom of rainbows.
Her home is filled with weavings of all colors and patterns.

6

She has spun them all on her spindle.
She has woven them all on her loom.

7

Her husband, the Sun, is pleased when he sees them.
It was She, Spiderwoman.

Spiderwoman taught White-Shell-Woman the secrets of weaving.
White-Shell-Woman watched Spiderwoman weaving on her rainbow loom.

For four days White-Shell-Woman watched.
White-Shell-Woman returned to her Earth Surface People.

10

There, she made a loom of wood and yarn.
There, she shared the secrets she had learned.

11

In this way the Earth Surface People received the gift of Kokyangwuti, the Spiderwoman.

12

The End

13

Toys and Games

Background Information

Children the world over play games to amuse themselves and to structure their time in a social setting. Children have the uncanny ability to create toys for themselves and for each other from whatever materials are available. For example, dolls have long been made from corn husks, sticks, and fabric scraps. Some games do not require any game pieces or objects. These are games which include physical activities such as foot races, swimming, jumping, or dancing, or nonsense games like the staring game in which two people stare at each other to see who will laugh first. Through words, songs, numbers, games, and physical activities, children can learn to communicate, share, take turns, and solve problems. Their reward for such activity is simple: they have fun.

The Importance of Play

Games are fun and encourage social interaction, the exhibition of skills, physical, verbal, and mental reinforcement by peers and adults, record-keeping, and awareness of sequential events. Children often learn as they play. They also reinforce their learning through the repetition of play.

Early Native American Play

This chapter describes games and toys from early North American cultures. Children of those times often played games which were an imitation of adult activities, such as baby-sitting, planting crops, basket-weaving, or hunting. The children imitated the behavior which was directly modeled by the parents or other adults and peers of the community. In early cultures, activities which the children approached as games were both enjoyable and educational.

Many of the things children did (or mimicked) in play were basic survival skills. These included starting fires for warmth and cooking, hunting or gathering plants such as nuts and wild berries, and distinguishing between edible and non-edible plants. The knowledge of medicinal plants such as plantain (which was used as an antidote to poison ivy) was highly valued. The medicine healers were men and women who possessed such knowledge and treated patients of all ages. Children could learn through play modelled after the work of the healers. Other skills which were learned through games and general play were the construction of temporary shelters and camping grounds, sewing and decorating clothes, weaving, and pottery.

Toys and Games *(cont.)*

Types of Games Played by Early Native American Children

There were many types of games across the American continent. Some of these games, such as foot-races, are still familiar to modern children. Some examples of traditional games played by early Native American children are as follows:

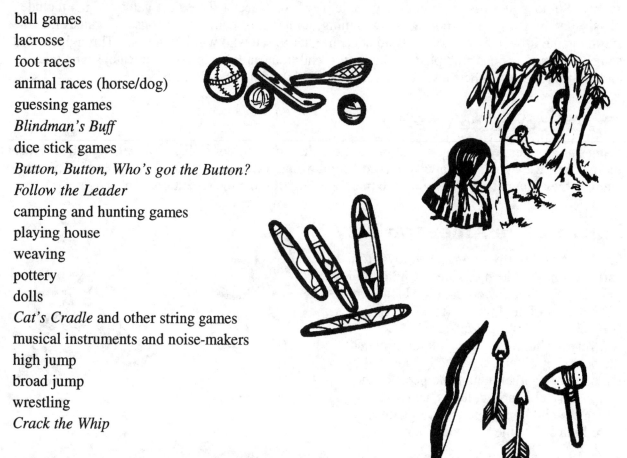

ball games

lacrosse

foot races

animal races (horse/dog)

guessing games

Blindman's Buff

dice stick games

Button, Button, Who's got the Button?

Follow the Leader

camping and hunting games

playing house

weaving

pottery

dolls

Cat's Cradle and other string games

musical instruments and noise-makers

high jump

broad jump

wrestling

Crack the Whip

Materials for Games and Toys

The materials which were available for the making of toys and games were many. They included: stones, clay, corn husks, seeds, leaves, sticks, animal bones, fur, animal hides, gourds, feathers, corncobs, berries, nuts, shells, pebbles, wood, bark, twine, and vines.

In order to make models of these traditional toys, the modern classroom can substitute tissue paper, dried macaroni, naugahyde, and synthetic furs for the natural materials.

Pages 166–176 provide basic instructions for traditional games, as well as worksheets and patterns for educational play. Some games presented in this chapter are modern games such as Tick-Tack-Toe which have been modified with images of early America.

Topics for Discussion

Discuss your favorite games and the traditional games of the early Native American children. Use some or all of the following questions as discussion topics.

1. What is a game? Which games can you name?
2. How old were you when you started to play games and play with toys?
3. What is your favorite game? What is your favorite toy? Why?
4. Why do we play games?
5. Do adults play games? What kind of games do adults play?
6. Do adults play with toys? What kind of "toys" do adults play with?
7. Do adults play games for the same reasons that children play?
8. What are your toys made from?
9. Where were your toys made? Who made them? How did you get them?
10. What kind of games did the early Native American children play?
    (ball games, lacrosse, foot races, guessing games, *Blindman's Buff*, dice-stick games, etc.)
11. Did they play any of the same games that are played today?
    (Yes, they played many games that are played today. See page 164.)
12. With what kinds of toys did the early Native American children play?
13. Who made these toys, and what were they made from?
    (The children themselves and their family members usually made the toys. They were made from whatever materials were naturally available.)
14. Have you ever made up a new game? Have you ever made your own toys?
15. Are there games and toys which children all over the world enjoy? Which ones? Why?

Traditional Games

Hide and Seek

This game varies regionally today and is sure to have varied among children of earlier times. However, the basics are always the same.

The player who is "It" closes his/her eyes and counts while the other players hide. When the counting is complete, "It" looks for the hiding places of the other players. The hiding players may have a "safe spot" to which they can run and not be "tagged." The first player to be found hiding and then "tagged" is the next player to be "It."

Miniature Toys

Native American children made small toys which looked like the tools, utensils, and hunting weapons of the adults. The children used sticks, reeds, grass, stones, feathers, and animal hides to make toy dolls, bowls, bows and arrows, axes, cutting knives, houses, and corn grinding stones. The children would then pretend to be on a hunting trip, building a campsite, or playing house. The dolls, of course, were family members.

Straw Bundles

This popular game took many forms. A dozen or more small reeds or sticks were tied together in a bundle. The players would then take turns pulling a handful of sticks from the bundle. The players tried to guess if the number of sticks which they held was even or odd. The player who was correct the most often was the winner. This game can be played with bundles of drinking straws or pencils if reeds and sticks are not handy.

Tag

This game had many versions. Usually, one player was chosen to be "It" and tried to catch or "tag" the other players. The first player to be "tagged" was "It" for the next game.

166

Traditional Games *(cont.)*

Ball Games

Ball games were popular with Native American children everywhere. Balls were made from sewn leather, stones, wood, grass, and rubber. Some of the ball games which were played were lacrosse, shinny, catch, tag ball, and hit the target. Lacrosse was an Iroquois game played with a small ball and a woven paddle. Shinny was played with a long pole as in ice hockey.

"Double ball" games were played with two balls joined by string and hit with a stick.

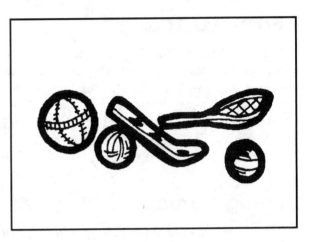

Dice Stick Games

Dice sticks and kicking sticks were made from wood or bone which was carved and painted with designs on one or both sides. Many games were played with decorated sticks. The four stick dice game was a patterns guessing game. Some painted sticks were tossed into the air and the pattern or number of sticks was guessed before the sticks fell. Larger sticks were kicked or thrown for long distances. The player whose stick covered the farthest distance was the winner. The small painted sticks were sometimes stored in a basket. (See page 171 for a dice stick activity.)

Dolls

Dolls were made by adults and children. Some dolls were dressed in sewn leather clothes or woven cloth. Human hair or horse hair was sometimes used for the dolls. Small jewelry and tiny toys were made for some dolls. Leather, ice, grass, sticks, mud, and stones were used to make doll houses. (See pages 172 and 173 for doll activities.)

Traditional Games (cont.)

Spinning Tops

Tops were made from wood, bone, stone, and clay. Most tops were small to fit a child's hand. Tops were sometimes carved and painted with colorful designs. Some tops were wound with rawhide string and "snapped" as they were released to spin. Players would see who could make the top spin for the longest time or for the farthest distance. (See page 174 for a top activity.)

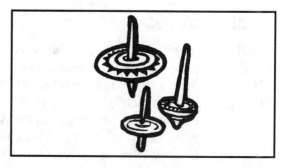

String Games

This game was played with long thin strips of sinew, leather, or yarn. One player held the yarn with both hands outstretched. Patterns were then formed step by step with the yarn. Poems and stories were sometimes narrated as the patterns changed. Adults and children enjoyed many versions of the string games. (See page 175 for *Cat's Cradle* directions and page 176 for the *Fish Spear* variation.)

Animal Races

Animal races were very popular. Observers tried to guess which animal would win the race. Dogs competed in running races in fair weather or sled races in the snow. Horseback riders competed to see which horse could run the farthest and the fastest. Some games were also played on horseback, such as target shooting with arrows and a game resembling polo with long sticks and a small ball.

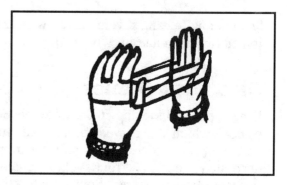

Instruments and Noise Makers

Early Native American children made instruments and noise makers. Small drums were made from clay, wood, and animal hide. Rattles of wood, shells, stones, gourds, and cactus stems were made to create rhythm for dancing. Grooved sticks, bells, and "bull-roarers" were made from wood, metal, rawhide, and stones. The instruments and noise makers were decorated with paint, carvings, feathers, and shells.

168

Traditional Games *(cont.)*

Foot Races

Many kinds of foot races were played by the children. Races were run to see who could run the farthest and the fastest. Obstacle course races could be very challenging, covering difficult terrain. Runners could be required to hop, skip rope, or jump as they ran. Racers could also move with their feet held behind them as they walked on their knees. Three-legged races were played just as they are today with two runners having one leg each bound together.

Miniature Basketry and Pottery

Young children imitated their elders by weaving small baskets from grass, twigs, and yarn. Some of these baskets had fitted tops. Tiny carrying baskets were made from scraps of birchbark or elm bark. Little dishes, bowls, and utensils of wood, stone, or clay were made for "cooking." Small pottery was made from clay. These miniature baskets and pots were decorated with paint, shells, and feathers. The miniature baskets and pottery were sometimes left as a "gift of thankfulness" for trees and plants which were used for food, medicine, or shelter.

Hide-the-Bean

This was a popular game with children and adults. Four painted bowls were placed in a row on the ground. The first player hid a small object under one of the bowls. This might be a stone, a button, a shell, or a bean. The second player tried to guess which bowl was covering the object.

This game can be played with decorated milk cartons or tin cans. Predictions and guesses may be recorded on a scorecard.

Dart Games

Many styles of dart games were played. The darts were often made from feathers and painted wood. The darts were thrown at a target which was made from a wooden hoop. The target hoops could be placed on the ground or upright against a rock. Adults also played dart games for fun and competition.

Traditional Games *(cont.)*

Miniature Animals

Children made small animals from scraps of animal hide, clay, sticks, grass corn husks, and cattail reeds. Small saddles, saddle blankets, and bridles were put on the toy horses. Miniature travois were made for the toy horses and dogs. Animal corrals were made from sticks to keep the animals from "running away."

Yo-Yo Games

Children of the Arctic made yo-yos by joining two pieces of fur together. A long thin strip of sinew was used for the string. The players would try to see who could make their yo-yos work for the longest time. Yo-yo tricks were practiced as well.

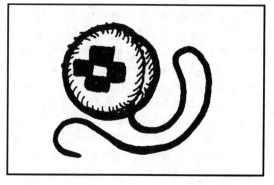

Fun With Feathers

Feathers were used in many ways. One feather game was played by two or more children to see who could keep his/her feather from falling to the ground by blowing air on it through a reed straw. Another game was to draw a line in the dirt and see who could first blow a feather across it. In yet another game, a feather was cupped in the hands and "blown" by one player. The other player tried to guess if the feather was still caught inside the first player's hands. All of these feather games are easy and safe to play indoors.

Dice Sticks

Children of the Great Plains played this game with painted wooden sticks.

Materials: stick patterns and scorecard (below), crayons, pencil, and scissors

Directions: Color and cut out the four dice sticks. Cut out the scorecard.

To play, Player A arranges the four sticks in a secret order and then covers the sticks with a piece of paper. Player B tries to guess the pattern of the four sticks. Players record their correct guesses on the scorecard. The player with the most correct guesses wins.

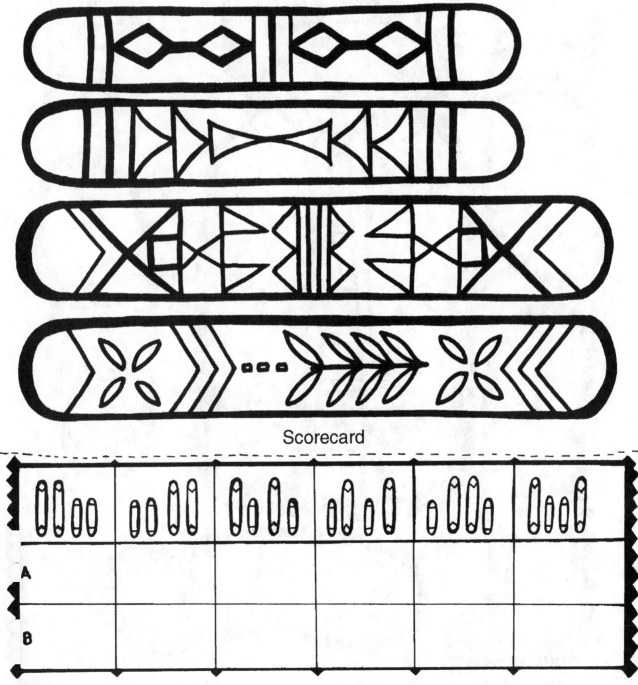

Scorecard

Arctic Doll

The Inuit children of the Arctic played with dolls sewn from leather and fur.

Directions: Color and cut out the Arctic doll pieces. Join the arms and legs to the body with brads.

Cornhusk Doll

Children of the Southwest made dolls from cornhusks and cattail reeds. Follow the steps below to make your own "cornhusk" doll.

Materials: scissors, yarn, crayons, and heavy crepe paper (or cornhusks)

Directions:

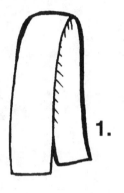

1.

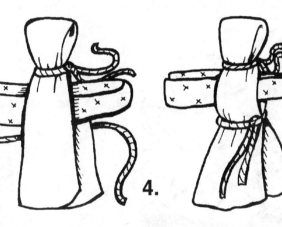

3.

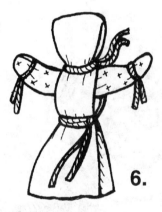

6.

5.

Spinning Tops

Children across North America made spinning tops from painted and carved wood and bone. Make your own spinning tops from the patterns below.

Materials: scissors, crayons, toothpicks, and a pencil

Directions: Design, color, and cut out the top patterns. Put a toothpick through the center of each and spin it.

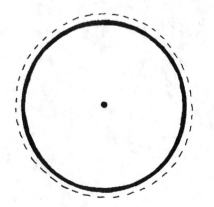

Cat's Cradle

Many early Native Americans enjoyed string games. These games were played by taking a long, thin strip of sinew, leather, or yarn in the hands and forming intricate pictures with it. One player held the yarn with both hands outstretched. Sometimes a second player pulled the yarn away and formed a new picture with a few hand moves.

Such string games are still popular today among children all over the world. To play *Cat's Cradle*, follow these directions.

Materials: 3' (1 m) piece of string

Directions:

1. Tie the ends of the string together. Start with the string looped around your thumbs and little fingers.

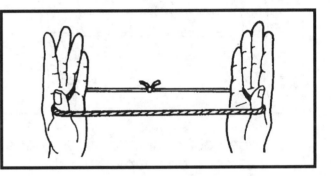

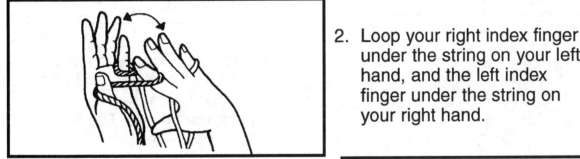

2. Loop your right index finger under the string on your left hand, and the left index finger under the string on your right hand.

3. Pull both hands apart. The string should look like the picture to the right.

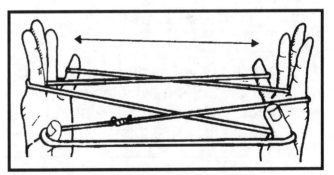

Make string pictures by looping the string over your hands and using your fingers to intertwine the string. You will find a *Cat's Cradle* variation called *Fish Spear* on the next page.

Fish Spear

Materials: 3' (1 m) piece of string

Directions:

1. Start with the string looped around your thumbs and little fingers.

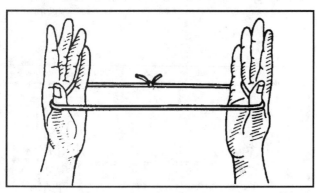

2. Loop your right index finger under the string on your left hand.

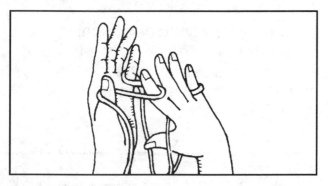

3. Twist it down away from you and up toward you twice as you pull your hands apart. The string should look like this:

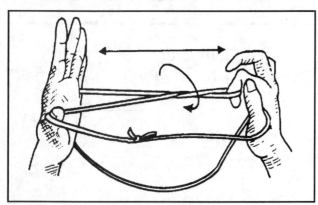

4. Pass your left index finger down through the loop over your right index finger and pick up the string that crosses your palm from underneath. Pull your hands apart. The string should look like this:

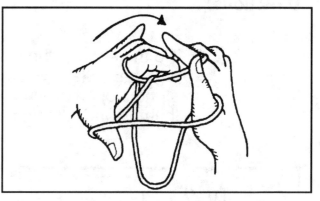

5. Release the loops from around your right thumb and little finger. Pull your right index finger to tighten the figure. The string should look like this:

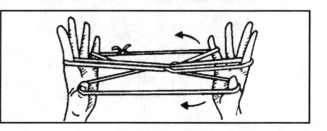

6. The three loops represent the three prongs of a fishing spear and the long loop is the spear itself.

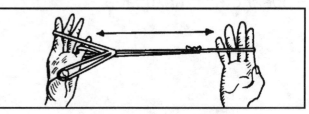